.net Guide #7

All you need to know about
Setting up a BBS

the internet magazine

.net

.net Guide #7

All you need to know about
Setting up a BBS
by Toby Simpson

Future Publishing Limited
Beauford Court
30 Monmouth Street
Bath
Avon BA1 2BW

.net Guide #7 All you need to know about Setting up a BBS
Copyright 1995 Future Publishing Limited. All rights reserved. No part of this
publication may be reproduced in any form except as permitted by the
Copyright Designs and Patents Act 1988. Enquiries for permission to reproduce
material should be directed to the publisher.

 Future Publishing Limited, Beauford Court, 30 Monmouth
Street, Bath, Avon BA1 2BW

ISBN 1-898275-37-8

British Library Cataloguing in Publication Data
A CIP catalogue record for this book is available from the British Library

Author Toby Simpson

Series Editor Davey Winder

Book Editor Rod Lawton

Book Design Rod Lawton

Subbing and layout Steve Faragher

Cover origination Nick Aspell

Printed and bound by Redwood Books

Contents

Chapter 3
What you will need

Chapter 4
Networks

Chapter 5
Making your BBS unique

Chapter 6
Legal issues

Chapter 7

Chapter 8

About the author

Toby Simpson is 25, unfit, and lives in a little house in
Cambridge, England. He writes computer games for a
living. His hobbies include (rather sadly) computers and
pinball, and he's not particularly good at the latter.
Fortunately an increasing interest in caving and climbing
offers a chance at redemption. He drinks abnormal amounts
of single malt Scotch whisky, has never met aliens, and has
yet to successfully grow any form of plant whatsoever. His
favourite dinosaur is a Stegosaurus, and he's a whole bunch
more interesting than he sounds. Probably.

Books by the same author

ARexx: Your Amiga's Built-In Turbocharger (the best ARexx
tutorial and reference guide you can buy, by the way).

.net Guide #1 *Getting On-Line*

Both are published by Future Publishing.

How to use this book

.net Guide #7 All you need to know about Setting up a BBS
is one of a series of Internet books designed to focus on the
needs of real Internet users. For a full list of the books in this
series – and details of other Internet publications we do –
see the back of this book.

All of our Internet books are written in plain English for
people who are more interested in the Net than computers.
And to make it even easier, we've included icons in the
margins to draw your attention to especially important
pieces of information. Here are the icons, together with an
explanation of what they mean (although it's all pretty
obvious):

 **Most of the things you read get stored away in your head
somewhere or other. When you see this icon, though,
make sure you store this item somewhere prominent!**

 **Top Tip. There are lots of ways of saving time, money
and effort that you'll never see in print. Except here!**

 **Anything to do with the Internet is packed with jargon.
You can't get rid of it, you just have to live with it...**

 **Warning! You won't see this icon too often, but when you
do, pay attention! Ignoring it could cost you time, money
or your sanity. And none of us have much to spare of any
of those.**

#7 Setting up a BBS **.net**

Foreword

A bulletin board, in its simplest form, is a piece of cork board stuck to the wall of your office where people can leave notes for everyone else to see. In computer terms, a bulletin board is just like this, a place where people can leave notes for other people to see. Only there is a catch, if you put a bulletin board on your computer at home, only the people in your house could use it. Not much fun, and certainly not likely to inspire any particularly amazing conversations. Computer based Bulletin Board Services (or BBSs) open themselves up to the world by using the telephone line, allowing people from anywhere around the globe to call in and use them.

In this book we'll show you how to set up your own BBS, and look at some of the issues you will have to deal with; such as the equipment you'll need; the software; and the sort of service that you will be expected to provide, as well as looking at legal aspects of storing data on your machine.

It's a complex business, but can be immensely rewarding if you get it right. I ran a BBS for a few years back in the late 80s, it had to close when I moved, but I had a great time doing it and may well have another go in the future.

I'd like to thank all those who have helped me with my research, especially Ian Moran and all the sysops I pestered late at night with silly questions! I'd also like to thank my family and friends, and Rod and Ian at Future Publishing for continuing to have faith in my writing and giving me more chances to write books, I'll become an author yet...

 .net Guide

How to get the most out of this book

Setting up a BBS is a very complex subject, and there is not necessarily a straightforward answer to anything, which makes writing a book of this kind very difficult. Some sections may not be entirely relevant to your BBS. If you already have some idea of what you want to achieve, we can help give you the information you need to go about setting it up. If you don't know, but just fancy the idea of running your own BBS (and why not?), then Chapter 2 will suggest services which a BBS operator may be expected to provide, and this can make an excellent starting point.

xii

 .net Guide

Chapter 1
Introduction

O ne of the problems with conventional telephone conversations is that they invariably take place at the convenience of one party. All too often, the other party is unable to answer the phone. They're in the bath, about to pop to a meeting, strolling to the shop for a snack, or just plain busy. It can become very frustrating to attempt to contact someone, leaving frequent messages, getting generally wound up and still failing totally to talk to the person you're after.

Then along came the fax machine. This neat device allowed you to send messages when you wanted to, and the person at the other end could read them whenever he or she was ready to. Fax machines still aren't perfect though. They don't allow you to hold discussions with lots of people, and there is the fiddling around with bits of paper. A far neater way to handle all this is electronically.

Electronic mail (email) has become increasingly popular both for corporate and private individuals as a fast, efficient way of sending information. Global communication networks such as the Internet have made it very easy to find answers to questions, get hold of just about anything you can imagine, and talk to people.

As we stroll towards the turn of the century, these networks carry more and more information, and it won't be long before you can watch movies and hold video-phone style conversations with people on the other side of the world. This rapid expansion has certainly not helped the private bulletin board operator.

In the early 80s it became possible for anyone to set up a bulletin board in their own bedroom. Armed with a

.net Guide

computer, a modem and a phone line, it was possible to set up an on-line service. With free local calls in a lot of places, private BBSs blossomed all over North America. People were able to talk to each other, send electronic mail, and have access to all sorts of goodies, from documents and pictures to computer games and utilities, with lots of weirder things in between.

Then computers got bigger. Suddenly a simple utility might be 250K in size. BBS operators with a bit of cash were able to add hard drives and CD-ROM drives to their systems. In addition larger, nation-wide networks were beginning to spring up, such as CompuServe and Cix. These services costed money to be a part of, but more information was available. This dragged a lot of users away from private BBSs. With so many BBSs to choose from, a BBS had to offer something unique or be overwhelmed by the opposition. Many BBSs closed or simply died out as the decade came to an end.

WARNING
It is surprising just how much patience, dedication and money you actually need to set up and run a BBS from scratch. With all of the depressing dialogue above, you may be just about ready to close this book and go to the pub instead. Well, don't. If you're seriously thinking about it, then read on.

Setting up a BBS is actually very straight forward; getting anyone to call it is not. In this book, we're not going to simply show you how to set a BBS up. We're going to discuss the kinds of services you may want to provide, the legal issues, and how to go about making your BBS unique from the others.

Why run a BBS?

What a good question! Why start a BBS? Well, if you've got as far as buying this book then you must have some idea as to the answer to this one.

My answer would be that it is great fun. It's a way to meet new people and learn a lot about computers and communications. There are a number of more specific answers, you may have a particular idea in mind, such as a theme, for example. It is important to sit down and think about what you wish to achieve, as setting up a unique dial-in BBS may not be the solution. If you want to provide an information service, about, say single malt scotch whiskies, you may be better off plugging yourself into the Internet and setting up some WWW pages, or an FTP service (see chapter 4 for more information on the Internet).

Bulletin boards tend to fall into two categories:

Open services

Open services are those which are available to the general public. Any user can connect to your BBS when they wish to, by either dialling up to it, or connecting through the Internet.

Open BBSs tend to be themed in some way, and cover a particular subject. This may be a computer, or something completely different. There are many thousands of open BBSs around the globe, and the successful ones are those which offer something that the others do not, or have particularly dedicated operators.

Closed services

Closed services are not available to the general public. Admission is strictly by permission of the operator. Some closed services are subscription based; you pay money to have access. Many of the world's conferencing systems work in this way. You pay money on a monthly basis to be connected. Delphi, CompuServe and CIX operate on this basis. The advantage is that the service provider is getting money, and is able to buy the right equipment and hire staff to develop and maintain the system.

Another kind of closed system can be a privately run BBS which you may set up just for a few friends to use. There are many systems like this, but it is difficult to justify spending the money and dedicating a phone line when you are only going to get a couple of calls a day.

MAKE A
NOTE!

It is important to know which category your BBS will fall into, as it will make a great deal of difference as you read this book. Its no bad idea to sit down with a piece of paper, a pen and write down exactly what you want to do and list the sort of services you wish to provide (use chapter 2 as a check-list).

What will it cost?

An obvious statement. In chapter 3 we will be looking at hardware and software that you may need. Depending on what you're planning on doing, this could cost you a little or a lot. If you already have a computer with a sizable hard drive, a modem and a phone line, then you could get up and running without spending any money at all. Of course, you pay in other ways.

Setting up a BBS is going to cost you a lot of time and effort, as after you have it up and running you have to support your users, and maintain your data; you never know what someone might say or do. "I didn't know it was there, officer" is not an excuse when the police break your door down and discover recipes for drugs, or pornographic material on your BBS, regardless of whether you knew it was there or not.

And BBSs are complex beasts, they rely on a lot of other bits and pieces to work reliably 24 hours a day, all of which will take a lot of effort from you. If your BBS is always breaking down for one reason or another (your modem hung, or your software crashed, or whatever) and people can never get through, they are going to get frustrated, and eventually give up. Your BBS is not the only one out there, and callers can afford to be picky – and will be.

It is often suggested that BBSs, like girlfriends, are a good way to get rid of any spare money you may have. Indeed, all of your money. You are unlikely to make any cash out of running a BBS, but you are going to have to spend plenty. Your reward is the satisfaction of seeing people out there choosing your service over someone else's, and the fun of running it. It's a great feeling of power!

What to expect

To brutally steal the RSPCA's slogan, remember, a BBS is not just for Christmas, it is for life. You can't really go into this

 .net Guide

half-heartedly, because that's the best way to guarantee that
everything will go horribly wrong. If you are going to run a
BBS, do it properly, or not at all, you'll save a lot of money
and time that way. Here are some thoughts to bear in mind:

Get a dedicated line
Many budding BBS operators think they can get away with
one phone line, by specifying a set range of times at which
people can call. At other times, the line will be used for
voice calls. Don't do this unless you're planning on
operating a small closed service where you know the people
who will call. BBS users have a tendency to forget these
times, and if they call from abroad, its quicker to just try
your number than work out if the timing is correct.

If you don't have a dedicated line, and don't operate 24
hours a day, you'll soon get fed up of picking up the phone
to the sound of a modem beeping at you. Installing a new
telephone line isn't really that expensive these days,
particularly if you are using a cable television phone line.
The moral of this bit is: "Get a dedicated line. Run your BBS
24 hours a day."

Once you've got started, it's hard to stop
There are two reasons why this is the case. Once you've got
a service running, and people are calling it, it is not very
pleasant to simply shut down the service at your whim. You
may think "hey, but it's my BBS. I'll do what I want", and
you'd be right. It is, and you can. But if you operate an
open system, and your BBS is successful, people may start
to rely on the service. It's not good manners to then pull the
rug out from underneath their feet, and after all, you
wouldn't like it if someone did it to you.

The other thing to consider is that once you've closed it,
you'll have to get the telephone number changed. Shutting
down a BBS takes a fair while. It may only take you 30
seconds: switch off the computer and disconnect the
modem. Job done. Unfortunately news travels slow, and
people maintain lists of BBSs and may not necessarily know
you have closed down. If you don't change the phone
number, or have the line disconnected, then you'll find it
will continue to ring for many months.

Running a BBS costs time and money

If your BBS is particularly successful, you may require
additional hard disks, or even more phone lines. (There is
nothing more irritating than not been able to get through
to a BBS for days because the line is always engaged.) So
bear in mind that if it goes well, you may be looking at
either spending more money or watching it all fall apart.

As well as that, a successful BBS requires regular support
from the operator. You'll be needed to answer queries,
upgrade and update your service, check files which have
been uploaded, validate new users, all sorts of things. And
this can easily be a process which can take at least an hour a
day. Think of your BBS as a spider plant. If you feed it well
and look after it, the thing will become huge and will need
re-potting. Which costs money. If you don't, it will die. If
you stop regularly feeding it, it may die also. But there is
something about seeing a strong healthy spider plant which
makes the hassle worth it. (Or maybe that's just me, and the
fact that spider plants are the only ones I appear to be able
to grow.)

There's no money in it

Unless you've got a lot of money, and a very, very good service, you are unlikely to be able to get away with charging users for a private system. There are many out there who don't charge, and people will simply not call yours. Just about the only way you can get away with it is if you offer a unique service which people will be prepared to pay for. And that's unlikely these days, with the Internet about.

If your BBS becomes larger, you may be able to charge a small amount for access to additional phone lines, or ask for donations from users to cover new hardware items, but don't bank on it.

What's my job, and what do I need to know?

Well, if you are setting up and then planning on running your own BBS, you are the system operator or "sysop". Your job is just that, to operate the system. This can involve a considerable range of tasks, from setting up new services (such as games, or Internet access, perhaps) to answering queries from users with problems. You are going to need lots of patience, not everyone is an expert.

I wouldn't recommend going into this with no technical expertise whatsoever. You should at least be familiar with what a modem is, and have used on-line services yourself already. I suggest if you are new to all of this that you invest in a suitable modem (see chapter 3), and start calling a few

This is how a modem
works, translating
electrical impulses into
audio signals at one end
and re-converting them
at the other.

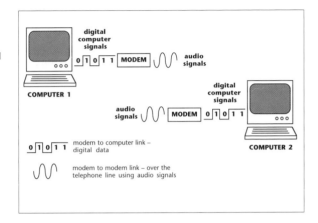

BBSs. Some numbers are included in chapter 7, call a few,
and get a feel for them and their users.

It sounds hard, where do I start?

With this book! It's not quite as hard as it may appear, so
long as you are reasonably organised and have a good idea
as to what you wish to do. As I suggested earlier, writing
down ideas for your BBS and calling other ones will help
give you a clearer idea of what services to provide yourself
in order to encourage people to call.

MAKE A
NOTE!

**Spend a few weeks thinking about it before going about
setting up your BBS. It's amazing how enlightening a bit
of thinking can be. After a few weeks of note taking you
should have generated a good specification for your BBS
and started to get a feel for its character. This will help
you to make it all happen, and buy the right kit without
wasting money on things that you don't need. I can't**

over-stress the importance of research. Look around,
have some fun, and call some **BBS**s.

When you get yours going, mail me and let me know at:

`toby@cix.compulink.co.uk.`

Two common setups

This is a question with several answers. It depends entirely
on the type of service you set up. Let's have a brief look at
the two most common setups.

Conventional dial-up service

This is where users of your BBS dial its phone number
directly. Normally callers would use a terminal package. This
means that when connected, every character they type on
their keyboard gets sent to your BBS software, and every
character you send back gets shown on their screen. They
get to interact directly with your service. Your BBS is

Logging on to a BBS.
Having typed our name and
password, we then have the
main menu, which shows
the choices we have.

This is a multi-user dungeon in Ireland. We are running around a world populated with other real people, there could be potentially hundreds of people playing this game at the same time as us!

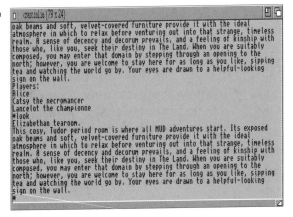

connected to a telephone using a modem, this device converts computer information into an audio signal which can be sent over the telephone line. This process is reversed at the other end, converting audio data back into computer information.

The BBS software on your system waits for the phone to ring, answers the call, and then starts communicating with the caller. Usually the caller has to sign on with a unique name and password before being granted entry. After this, the caller navigates your BBS using commands, or a set of menus. When the caller is finished, the BBS disconnects from the line and waits for the next call to arrive.

Internet or direct network connection

This is considerably more complex than a direct dial-up service, and is much harder to set up. It also has the potential to be more expensive, as for users to be able to connect at any time, you have to be attached to the Internet, or another network, all of the time. With cheap, cable TV-based phone lines, and local Internet access points,

it is just beginning to come into people's reach. Chapter 4
looks into network connections in much more detail.

Usually this type of setup also requires a modem. Instead of
sending and receiving simple text information, data is
transferred in special packets which are decoded at each
end. The user cannot connect using a simple terminal
program, and will require more complex software. At your
end, you'll need to have software to deal with the network
connection, and provide services.

In the case of the Internet, this normally involves TCP/IP
networking software (see chapter 4) and a number of
additional packages to give callers access to features such as
conferencing, email, games and other goodies. The
advantage with a setup like this is that it is easier to support
more than one user at once without having to buy
additional telephone lines, as the data-packets have
information inside them describing where they came from
and where they are going.

Chapter 2

Services you will be expected to provide

In this chapter we will look at the sorts of services which you can provide on your BBS. What you actually choose will depend greatly on the type of BBS you intend to provide. Specialised information services, for example, are unlikely to require conferencing facilities. If you're planning on setting up a closed system for just a few of your friends, then you may only need email and a couple of other things. It is not reasonable to expect that you will provide all of the services described in this chapter, at least not at first!

Electronic mail

Electronic mail is just that, letters which are sent electronically. Some email systems allow pictures and sounds to be embedded into messages, but the most common email consists of just text. This is one of the most common facilities which almost all BBSs provide, as it allows users to talk to each other privately.

Email in a closed environment is limited. If your BBS only allows mail to be sent to users on your BBS, then it is unlikely to be used for general purposes. Email comes into its own when you can link your email to other networks. Chapter 4 looks into networks such as Fidonet, and the Internet in greater detail. If you provide Internet mail access, for example, then users on your system suddenly have access to 30 million users world wide, both for sending and receiving mail. Almost all major world-wide services, commercial and private, provide some Internet connectivity, and this is the most important.

The Lucy Cix OLR. This software provides a GUI for access to the Cix subscription service. We can use it to send mail messages to anyone in the world. Here we see a message to Davey Winder, the series editor for these books!

When choosing which software to use for your **BBS**, it is worth checking if it provides a method of receiving mail from other networks, and sending it out. Of course, if you intend to write your own software (no small undertaking), then this is your problem!

Many text-based email systems now support limited text formatting using special character sequences. For example, a number of common services allow bold, italics and underlined to be specified. Text you want to appear in bold is simply surrounded with asterisks – *this is bold* would appear in bold text for example. The advantage of a system like this, is that if your mail reader does not support it, messages still look sensible.

If you decide that email is an important feature for you, it is worth ensuring that the software you use to run your BBS does a good job. Users may wish to pre-prepare long messages before dialling your BBS, and will want to be able to send these somehow. Check that your BBS software has a good text editor for users.

Internet access

It is unlikely that the Internet has escaped your notice in recent times. The Internet is a vast international network of computers. It consists of lots of smaller networks, all talking to each other. It is estimated that 30 million people use the Internet for one reason or another. This figure is growing rapidly. In 1994, the Internet was growing by 10% a month.

It is the sheer size of the Internet which makes it attractive to its users. No matter what information you want to find, the chances are extremely high that you can find it on the Internet. Internet email seems to hold the world's electronic mail system together these days. You can mail 30 million people, plus people on totally different networks such as CompuServe, BIX and Cix, and that's very attractive to your potential users.

What does this mean to BBS operators? Think of the Internet as a resource. If your BBS software is capable of interfacing to it, you can selectively give your callers access to certain Internet features. The primary one of use is Internet mail, as it opens your BBS up to the world.

What is the Internet for? Future Publishing's "All you need to know about the Internet", by Davey Winder, or .net guide #1 "Getting On-Line" are good books to give you an introduction to what the Internet is all about.

 .net Guide

**FTP in action, direct to a
site in North America**

```
ncftp>cd Fringe
wiretap.spies.com:/Library/Fringe
ncftp>dir
total 8
druxr-xr-x  2 wiretap  files      512 Jul  1 1993 .cap
-rw-r--r--  1 wiretap  files      290 May  4 1993 .files
druxr-xr-x  3 wiretap  files     1024 Jul 17 08:30 Conspiry
druxr-xr-x  3 wiretap  files      512 Jul  1 1993 Gross
druxr-xr-x  3 wiretap  files     1024 Jul  1 1993 Occult
druxr-xr-x  3 wiretap  files      512 Jul  1 1993 Pharm
druxr-xr-x  3 wiretap  files     1024 Jul  1 1993 Ufo
druxr-xr-x  3 wiretap  files     1024 Jul  1 1993 Weird
wiretap.spies.com:/Library/Fringe
ncftp>cd Weird
wiretap.spies.com:/Library/Fringe/Weird
ncftp>dir
total 464
druxr-xr-x  2 wiretap  files      512 Jul  1 1993 .cap
-rw-r--r--  1 wiretap  files     1419 May  4 1993 .files
-rw-r--r--  1 wiretap  files    17815 Dec 21 1992 bizarre.gan
-rw-r--r--  1 wiretap  files     1024 Sep 22 1988 bizarre.txt
-rw-r--r--  1 wiretap  files     4553 Sep 19 1988 bob.pic
-rw-r--r--  1 wiretap  files     3412 Sep 18 1988 byrne.txt
-rw-r--r--  1 wiretap  files    16940 Dec  3 1992 carboni.nf
-rw-r--r--  1 wiretap  files    17602 Dec  1 1992 chaos.def
-rw-r--r--  1 wiretap  files     4395 Sep 23 1989 citynine.txt
-rw-r--r--  1 wiretap  files    19243 Mar  3 1993 gavins.txt
-rw-r--r--  1 wiretap  files     5635 Dec  5 1992 hedgehog.sng
-rw-r--r--  1 wiretap  files    52173 Jan  6 1993 kibo.sig
-rw-r--r--  1 wiretap  files    16359 Dec 23 1992 kibology.faq
-rw-r--r--  1 wiretap  files    11651 Dec  4 1992 kibology.lis
-rw-r--r--  1 wiretap  files    10956 Feb  2 1993 kloo.txt
-rw-r--r--  1 wiretap  files     3584 Sep 22 1988 livesex.txt
-rw-r--r--  1 wiretap  files    13856 Sep 22 1988 madscrib.3
-rw-r--r--  1 wiretap  files    10640 Dec  5 1992 pagan.sng
-rw-r--r--  1 wiretap  files    11870 Dec 26 1988 pendrago.txt
-rw-r--r--  1 wiretap  files    12991 Oct  5 1988 recurse.txt
-rw-r--r--  1 wiretap  files     9705 Nov 23 1992 silicon.txt
-rw-r--r--  1 wiretap  files    52957 Oct 24 1992 summer.vac
-rw-r--r--  1 wiretap  files     5394 Apr 25 1988 warfare.txt
-rw-r--r--  1 wiretap  files    83677 Dec 19 1992 weird.nai
-rw-r--r--  1 wiretap  files    77377 Dec 21 1992 xibovac.txt
wiretap.spies.com:/Library/Fringe/Weird
ncftp>
```

As a BBS operator you should certainly be aware of the Internet and some of the basic features which it can offer you and your BBS callers. The following list covers the main ones which are most likely to be of interest to a BBS operator:

○ **FTP. File Transfer Protocol.** FTP is a system allowing files to be moved from any machine on the Internet to any other, security permitting. There are many computers on the Internet which provide public FTP access. This means you don't need a password and username to access it. There are tens of thousands of files covering every subject you could think of (and I'm not kidding, I thought of some *real* strange ones, and found them!).

Providing FTP access to your BBS can be a real boost. Suddenly, you don't have to have several Giga-bytes of hard drive space to store files, as users can go out and get them from the Internet.

○ **Telnet.** Telnet is very close to the heart of a BBS operator. It is effectively a Terminal program for the Internet. It allows

The World Wide Web in
action.

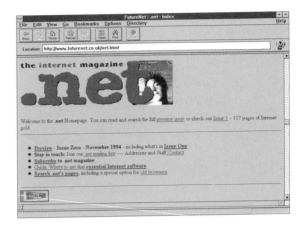

users to "log in" to computers on the Internet as if they
were connected with a conventional direct dial up link, i.e.,
calling a BBS. Telnet is often used for running BBSs on the
Internet, and for access to multi-user games such as
dungeon adventures.

○ **Archie and WAIS (Wide Area Information Server).**
With so much data on the Internet, one of the least
amusing things is actually finding anything in particular.
Archie and WAIS have evolved to help you to find files.
Archie does a file-name search, you can specify part of a file,
and it will then go off and find any matches and then list
the FTP sites at which they are available. WAIS goes one
step further, it actually looks inside individual documents
and tries to find specified keywords. It then builds a "high-
score" table of the most likely documents which are of
interest to you.

○ **Gopher and WWW (World Wide Web).** Gopher and
WWW are simply ways of navigating the Internet. Both are
most often used to find information on particular subjects.
Both are neat front ends to services such as Archie, WAIS,

 .net Guide

FTP and Telnet. Gopher came along first, and provides a menu driven approach, whereas the WWW, which is growing in popularity at an incredible rate, is hypertext style

○ **Usenet News.** Usenet is the Internet answer to a public conferencing system. We'll look at conferencing facilities in greater detail below. Usenet is a neat solution allowing people to hold conversations on a variety of different subjects while keeping them separated. Each individual conference is called a newsgroup. There may be several newsgroups on any given subject. Currently there are several thousand newsgroups, with subjects ranging from the martial arts to dentistry.

Providing access to Usenet newsgroups on BBSs is a popular addition. Most BBSs which implement any Internet access at all provide this and email. The only catch is that it can get expensive for you, as you have to receive the newsgroups from an Internet feed.

Two notes of caution about the Internet

Legal issues

The Internet is big, it is international, and it is *not policed*. The laws on pornographic material, amongst other things, differ from country to country, and it is easy to receive information that is totally illegal in this country without realising it. Chapter 6 covers legal issues in greater detail.

Costs

If you are providing any form of Internet gateway, you will
require a direct Internet feed of some sorts, and this will
cost you money. Furthermore, to receive Internet
information you will need to connect to your feed by
dialling out. Providing facilities like FTP "live" (i.e., the user
can use FTP immediately at request, rather than asking for it
to be sent at a later date) requires a separate line and
modem to call out, again at your cost.

On top of all this, your BBS software will need some way of
accessing the Internet, so you'll need to bear this in mind
when choosing your BBS package (see chapter 3).

To minimise costs, you can limit the types of Internet access
available. But be further warned: If you provide just email,
for example, be wary of the size of some messages which
can be moved around. One of your callers could ask for a
file to be FTP'd by mail. You can end up with 1Mb email
messages floating around, which you have to receive from
your Internet service provider yourself. This can be
extremely expensive.

Other network access: Fidonet

Fidonet first appeared on the scene in 1984, and was
designed as a means of transferring mail and files between
BBSs. As a network it is quite neat, all the transferring of
data is done at the dead of night when it is cheap. It quickly
took off with private BBSs as *the* network to connect to.
Currently, there are over 30,000 members of Fidonet, and
most of these are BBSs. Indeed, the chances are very high

that if you log onto any BBS these days, it will be connected to Fidonet.

So, what does it offer you and your user? Well, firstly it is relatively easy to get sorted out. There is a lot of software available designed to interface to Fidonet, and designed to plug into BBS software.

Your user is able to mail anyone on Fidonet, and this is a sizable bunch of people, from all over the world. They are also able to participate in conversations about certain subjects. Most of these are of a computing nature, with a strong emphasis on the PC and the Amiga.

The advantage of Fidonet over the Internet for BBSs, is that Fidonet is designed to be used over BBSs. It is also less crowded than the Internet, and in general, sizably cheaper to provide access to, for you and your users.

If you are interested in Fidonet and want to get hold of some more information then it is covered in more detail in chapter 4.

Conferencing facilities

If you choose to connect your BBS to a network such as the Internet or Fidonet, you will already be providing your users with some sort of conferencing facility. Think of a conference as a separate house on a long street. Each of these houses has a bunch of people in it wanting to talk about a certain subject. So, for example, if you wanted to talk about single malt scotch whiskies, you might walk into a conference specially for that. Sometimes, conferencing

Conferencing facilities, in this case on Cix, a commercial system .

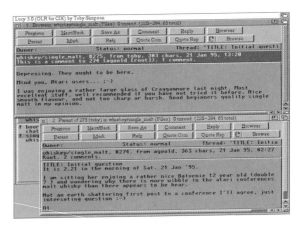

systems break this down further, and have sub-topics within a conference. A conference about the PC, for example, may be broken down into software, communications, hardware, and so on.

MAKE A
NOTE!

Each network and BBS package has a nasty habit of referring to conferencing by different names. The Internet conferencing facility is called Usenet news, Fidonet refers to it as echo mail.

Your BBS software, if it is worth its weight in anything, will support some form of conferencing. This will allow you to group chatter on certain subjects and keep them separate. It is also possible in some cases for you to restrict access to certain conferences to named people. This can be handy if you wish to discuss items of a private nature with a small group of people. You can also then do the same with your files, rather than having them all in one big lump. This makes it easier for your users to find anything on a given subject.

If your BBS is connected to Fidonet, you will be able to have echo mail areas of your choice also available to the user, so long as your BBS software supports it of course (see chapter 3 for more on that).

File areas

Most BBSs provide a bunch of files which are available for users to download. This is the area of BBSs which directly leads to you emptying out your wallet and handing the contents to someone else, normally in return for yet another large shiny hard drive. It doesn't take a mathematician to work out that if you have 1000 files available for users to download, at an average size of 80K, you'll need 80Mb of space. This doesn't sound like much, but depending on the types of files, this figure can leap up dramatically.

If your BBS focuses on 3D rendering then you may have a few hundred JPEG picture files, maybe a list of 3D models, then you may be talking about a gigabyte. Successful BBSs tend to have lots of files available. This costs you money, and if you don't have the finances to expand when the need arises, users may become frustrated at not being able to upload further files to your BBS and may go elsewhere.

The space you are going to require varies considerably with the type of BBS service you are providing. If you are joining 95% of most other BBSs, you'll be wanting to make PD software available. One way of making this cheaper is to have a CD-ROM drive and just keep updating the CD which is in it. This does not allow users to upload new files, but does mean that what hard drive space you *do* have can be

The file areas of a UK based
BBS, showing how good
organisation is very
important..

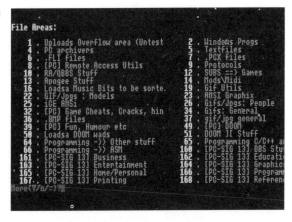

```
File Areas:

  1 . Uploads Overflow area (Untest      2 . Windows Progs
  4 . PC archivers                       5 . Textfiles
  6 . .FLI files                         7 . .PCX files
  8 . [PC] Remote Access Utils           9 . Protocols
 10 . RA/QBBS Stuff                      12 . SUBS ==> Games
 13 . Apogee Stuff                       14 . Mods\Midi
 16 . Loadsa Music Bits to be sorte.     19 . Gif Utils
 22 . GIF/Jpgs : Models                  23 . ANSI Graphix
 25 . iCE ANSi                           26 . Gifs/Jpgs: People
 32 . [PC] Game Cheats, Cracks, hin      34 . Gifs: General
 36 . .BMP files                         37 . gif/jpg general
 39 . [PC] Fun, Humour etc               49 . [PC] DOOM
 50 . Loadsa DOOM wads                   51 . DOOM II Stuff
 64 . Programming ->> Other stuff        65 . Programming C/C++ a
 66 . Programming ->> ASM               160 . [PC-SIG 13] BBS Stu
161 . [PC-SIG 13] Business              162 . [PC-SIG 13] Educati
163 . [PC-SIG 13] Entertainment         164 . [PC-SIG 13] Graphic
165 . [PC-SIG 13] Home/Personal         166 . [PC-SIG 13] Program
167 . [PC-SIG 13] Printing              168 . [PC-SIG 13] Referen
More(Y/n/=)?
```

used for this purpose and not be wasted with stacks of other junk.

As soon as you accumulate a decent amount of files, your BBS will start to become open to a certain level of abuse. It is very common for people to call your BBS, download a bunch of files, and then disconnect having contributed nothing whatsoever. Indeed, their only contribution is to tie up the phone line for legitimate users for astronomical lengths of time. This may not be a problem for you if your BBS exists to provide files to people, but as time edges on people who want that level of file access are heading in droves for the Internet because there are millions of files available, more than any private BBS could hope to provide, even with a month of Sundays and a serious lottery win.

One way around this is to give users a limit to the amount they can download in any 24 hour period, or to provide an upload to download ratio, where for every 1Mb downloaded at least 100K has to be uploaded (again, open to abuse, all sorts of junk could be uploaded to get around this). There are few ways to make even a cent out of

 .net Guide

running a BBS, but this is one. If users want to get rid of their download restrictions, or their upload to download ratio, you should encourage them to send you a fiver or something.

WARNING

A major consideration when providing files is the legal aspects involved. See chapter 6 for more information on this. Storing and distributing some types of information electronically is illegal, and you can get in a great deal of trouble if you are not careful. Make sure you understand the law and what you can and can't do, and you can sleep easier knowing that the police are not about to break down your door and confiscate your BBS (don't laugh; it happens regularly).

As mentioned in the bit about conferencing above, you can group files into subjects. This is a great way of reducing the lists users have to search through to find anything. A lot of BBS software allows these file areas to be tagged to particular conference groups, so in the chatter about Amiga, you will find the list of available Amiga files.

Games

BBS games can be great fun, particularly if they can support loads of players. The coolest thing about a lot of these multi-user games is that they do not require everybody playing to be connected at any one time, they tend to be turn based. This means that everyone has their turn when it is convenient for them, and at a set time regularly (daily, for instance) your computer will process everyone's turns for them and the game moves on.

You wouldn't believe it, but you can even play Tetris over a BBS. This version allows you to play against the sysop of the BBS you are calling also!

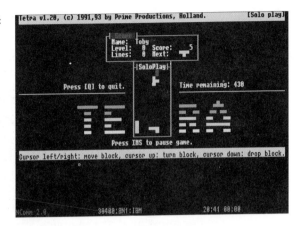

Most of these games are in the shape of add-ons, so you will need to check that your BBS software can support them (see chapter 3 for a look at BBS software).

There are also games which support multiple players at once. These are only relevant if you've got the time to play games with your caller, or if you have multiple lines and can support many calls at once, so tend to be less popular. And of course, there are games for single players, but you won't get too many people spending much time on those as they are running up their phone bill and could easily play those same games on their own computer and save money.

Multi-user chat

This is a sort of live conferencing for more than one person at once. At its simplest form it is a way for users to talk directly to the sysop. Most BBS software supports this ability at least, and it is a good way of answering specific problems or just having a chat and getting to know someone a bit better.

Chatting to Thomas, one of the many sysops who helped me with my research.

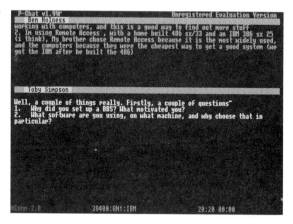

```
P-Chat v1.99r                                    Unregistered Evaluation Version
     Ben Holness
working with computers, and this is a good way to find out more stuff
2.  Im using Remote Access , with a home built 486 sx/33 and an IBM 386 sx 25
(i think), My brother chose Remote Access because it is the most widely used,
and the computers because they were the cheapest way to get a good system (we
got the IBM after he built the 486)


     Toby Simpson

Well, a couple of things really. Firstly, a couple of questions"
1.   Why did you set up a BBS? What motivated you?
2.   What software are you using, on what machine, and why choose that in
particular?



NComm 2.0              38400:8N1:IBM                    20:20 00:00
```

If your BBS has more than one phone line, then multi-user chat can really become fun as loads of people can all get together for a natter. On large networks such as the Internet this can become really amazing, as hundreds of people can get together (the most popular Internet form of multi-user chat is called IRC – Internet relay chat). If you are likely to end up with heaps of lines then you can group this down into conversations on certain subjects to keep them all separate, but unless you've got ten or more lines this is unlikely to be a concern.

A realistic setup

The above list is not remotely exhaustive, and there are many other things BBSs can do which you'll learn as you explore a bit and see what other BBSs offer. A list on its own is all well and good, it helps you choose which to provide, but if you're a beginner then it probably looks daunting and it can be hard to decide where to start.

What you should choose depends greatly on your BBS and the types of subjects you will be focusing on. Lots of BBSs are able to have a comfortable existence supporting only three of the above (conferencing, mail and files) and no network connections at all, simply because they cover a very closed subject range and don't need them.

If you set up your BBS to have file areas, some sort of conferencing and mail between users then that can be more than sufficient to get going. Fidonet is a serious consideration though as it is very popular for BBS users.

Chapter 3

What you will need

S etting up and running a bulletin board requires a lot of things, both material and non-material, ranging from patience to a modem. In this section we look into some of those requirements in greater detail, suggesting some of the hardware and software you may like to look at.

It is assumed that you are going to be using a modem and a telephone line rather than a direct network connection using a leased line. The latter is not only expensive, but highly complex, and would require a .net guide of its own to explain. The money required is sufficient to put it well out of the budgets available for most people setting up a private BBS (unless you've just won the lottery). The hardware goodies you will require are;

○ A suitable computer

○ A modem

○ A telephone line

○ Cables and connectors

○ Backup hardware

We'll look at each of these in turn later on. In addition to hardware requirements, you'll also need suitable software. There is much available, from freeware and shareware to the commercial packages, and of course, there is nothing stopping you from writing your own (unless you can't program!). We'll look at several software packages for the IBM PC and compatibles, Amiga and the Macintosh.

Armed with the appropriate goodies, you can then set about getting up and running. There are a couple of other things you'll need, which are worth mentioning. Patience is one of them. This is a time consuming thing to do, and you are likely to have plenty of problems to keep you busy. You'll also need a dash of dedication. Once your BBS is on-line, you'll need to spend time keeping it all going and providing support to your users.

The hardware

A suitable computer

What is a suitable computer? Well, for most people, it will be an IBM PC, a Macintosh, or an Amiga. It is unrealistic to expect to run a BBS without a hard drive. If you are planning on allowing users to upload and download files, then you'll be needing quite a large hard drive. Half a gigabyte is maybe even too small, but would certainly make a good starting point. Make sure your computer allows you to add extra hard drives at a later point. You may wish to consider having a CD-ROM drive as well.

Different BBS software packages put different demands on a system. Some PC software, for example, may require 8 or 16Mb of RAM. As a general rule, for PC, Macintosh and Amiga owners, here is the typical minimum specification system you will require to operate a BBS:

IBM PC and compatibles

○ 486 Processor

○ MS-DOS 6. You may also require Windows 3.1 depending on the software you choose

○ 8Mb of RAM

○ VGA card

○ large, fast hard-drive

Macintosh
○ 68030 Processor

○ System 7.0 software (Preferably 7.5 which is generally smoother)

○ 4Mb of RAM minimum

○ large, fast hard-drive

Amiga
○ 68020 Processor

○ Amiga OS 2.04 at least

○ 4Mb of RAM

○ large hard drive

You may actually be able to get away with less than this, but that would involve using older software which was designed in the days when computers were a mite littler. Although this is not a problem with PCs, Amiga and Mac users will need to seriously consider having a "box machine" which is able to take additional expansion cards

inside it. If you are planning to provide a BBS service for more than one caller at a time, you may need additional serial (COM) ports to plug more modems into.

A modem

If you're running a BBS, a modem is obviously an important piece of kit. It is the device which allows you to connect your computer to the outside world. The best advice I can give when choosing a modem is to buy the best one you can, budget permitting. Modern modems are capable of moving over 7K of text data per second over the phone line, and if one of your callers has such a modem, he or she will be a bit upset if it can't be used on your BBS.

So what are you looking for?
○ It should do at least 9600bps (bps – bits per second), which in this case it works out at about 1K per second without compression. 14400bps is better still. These speeds should be achieved using the ITU-T (see below for an explanation) 9600bps V32 standard and 14400bps V32bis standard. If you've got the money then seriously consider V34 modems (28800 bps) if they are available, or VFC (also 28800 bps).

○ It must be Hayes compatible (I'd be most surprised if you could find a modem that wasn't these days, but you never know!). It is also worth ensuring that the modem supports both auto-answer and auto-dialling. With some BBS software, auto-answer is not strictly necessary, as it detects the "RING" message from the modem and issues an "answer call now" instruction.

○ It should support automatic error correction, using the ITU-T V42 specification.

○ It should support data compression using ITU-T V42 bis. This will more than double the speed of your modem when transferring certain kinds of easily compressible data (such as text).

○ It must be BT approved. This may sound silly, but if it isn't, not only can you get into trouble should anyone ever discover (which I admit, is seriously unlikely), but it means that it has not been checked to ensure that it adheres to all of the UK telephone network specifications.

WHAT DOES IT MEAN

ITU-T: In the early 80s, manufacturers in many countries made modems which were compatible with the local phone networks. The result of this was a terribly confusing mixture of strange "standards". A set of official standards was set by an European body called the CCITT. This has now been replaced by the ITU-T (International Telecommunications Union – Telecommunications). The ITU-T is responsible for a set of 'V' standards. V34, for example, is the standard for modems to talk to each other at 28800 bits per second.

Other things to consider are the connections to your phone and computer. The modem should come with a standard DB-25 female connector on the back to plug into the computer, and a socket for you to connect it to the telephone line. (In some cases the telephone wire is moulded to the modem itself, with a phone connector at the other end – which is a bit awkward should the cable become damaged, as it becomes a very expensive repair job suddenly.)

If you wish to keep your telephone plugged in, then the modem you buy should have a pass-through telephone socket on the back. If it doesn't, this is no real hardship, pop into your local BT shop, or electrical store, and buy a one to two socket splitter so that you can plug the modem in at the same time as the phone. The only catch with this method is that the modem can't prevent you from picking up the phone while it's using the line, so you'll just have to be careful.

As well as external modems, you can also buy internal modems which plug inside your PC. These are convenient for PC owners who are a bit short of desk space, but are a hassle to install, and it's a pain to then move your modem to another machine. And, worst of all, should you change to a different computer, say from a PC to a Macintosh, then you'll have to sell the modem. External modems offer the greatest flexibility, but normally cost about 5% more than their internal counterparts.

Although I wouldn't recommend it in a million years, it is possible to run a BBS using a notebook computer. If you have one with a PCMCIA socket, you can buy small modems which plug into it. These tend to be a little expensive, but will usually run off the notebook's power supply, or battery. (For those with obscene amounts of money, modern GSM digital mobile phones are now available with PCMCIA cards which act as modems over the mobile phone line. Your own mobile BBS!)

So, with this in mind, let's look at some possible modems. This is certainly not an exhaustive list, if you would like to look at some other options, a magazine such as Futures ".net" should be able to help you. The costs shown here are the recommended retail prices, but these are rarely charged. Heavy discounting takes place on modems, so as well as the RRP we'll give you an idea of what you can realistically expect to pay. Although we mentioned approved modems in the previous section, it's worth mentioning this again, as you may find modems which look very cheap indeed and have all the features of something twice the price: the chances are that such modems will not be BT approved. Connecting non-approved modems to the BT telephone network is *illegal*. And as the operator of a BBS it is *not* worth the risk.

US Robotics

US Robotics produce a wide range of modems which are suitable for use on a BBS. An ideal one is the Sportster 14,400 FAX Modem. Okay, so it looks ugly, but it's cheap, reliable and very popular.

A nice added extra is the FAX capability, which won't help you run a BBS, but is nice to have. The Sportster 14,400 FAX Modem retails at £199 excluding VAT (that's £233.83 including VAT). US Robotics can be contacted on 01753 811180.

If you've got a few more pennies to spend, you might like to consider their 28,800 modems which use the VFC interim standard, or preferably V34 which is the official ITU-T standard for 28,800 bps modems. US Robotics also produce modems which use their own proprietary standard called

Typical modem cables. This picture shows you the ideal wires to connect for a PC or Amiga modem cable. Mac cables are a bit more of a pain, as the connectors are harder to get hold of.

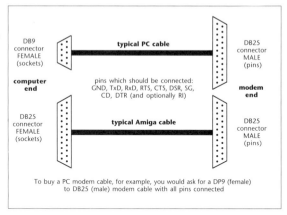

DB9 connector FEMALE (sockets)

typical PC cable

DB25 connector MALE (pins)

computer end

pins which should be connected:
GND, TxD, RxD, RTS, CTS, DSR, SG,
CD, DTR (and optionally RI)

modem end

DB25 connector FEMALE (sockets)

typical Amiga cable

DB25 connector MALE (pins)

To buy a PC modem cable, for example, you would ask for a DP9 (female) to DB25 (male) modem cable with all pins connected

HST, but modems that support HST as well cost a little more.

Hayes

Since all modems these days are Hayes compatible, it makes sense to mention Hayes as a modem manufacturer! Hayes have been in the business for a long time, and produce a wide range of very high quality modems. You can contact Hayes on 01252 775550 and ask for your local dealer, or further information.

Pace

Pace are another long-standing modem company, their tiny MobiFAX modem, for example, costs only £99 excluding VAT. It supports speeds of up to 14,400 and is approved for UK use. You can contact Pace on 01274 532000.

WARNING

A final note about modems. Having got one, the chances are very high that you'll need to buy the cable which connects your computer to the modem. The reason that this is not usually supplied with the modem itself, is that every computer has a different connector. PCs, for

example, have male **DB-9s, Amigas usually have male DB-25s, and Macs have their own unique connector! Check if a cable comes with your modem which is suitable and, if not, make sure you get one which supports hardware handshaking: CTS/RTS. Without this sort of cable you will run into serious problems using your modem later on. Such a cable should cost about £15 to buy, or about £3 to build yourself.**

A telephone line

You may already have one of these, which you use for voice calls. I'm afraid you'll need another. You'll regret it intensely if you don't run your BBS off a dedicated telephone line. If you are sharing your voice line with your BBS for incoming calls, you'll need to have specified times when users can call. Unfortunately, people will ignore or forget these times and call anyway and you'll have to pick up the phone to a computer regularly. Getting an additional telephone line installed is not that expensive, and can be done very quickly. If you use a cable TV based telephone service, you may find that additional lines can be added for a very small surcharge and monthly fee.

The only other thing to consider with phone lines is if you are planning on having more than one. If you intend on supporting many users at once, and you are not going to be running your BBS as an Internet connection (which is rare), then for every caller you wish to support simultaneously, you'll need another line. If your BBS becomes popular, you may need to do this. With cable TV phone lines, adding

more is a very simple and cheap option. There are a few
things to bear in mind:

○ If you ever want to have more than one line, your BBS
software needs to be able to support this. On multi-tasking
machines such as the Amiga most BBS software is capable
of handling many calls at once.

○ Each phone line will require its own modem. You may
end up with a whole pile of modems. And each modem
requires a spare serial port on your computer to plug into.
PC owners can add additional serial ports (or COM ports, as
they're known) very cheaply indeed. Amiga and Macintosh
owners can buy cards which plug into their machines to
add new serial ports. Of course, you will need a machine
which can have cards plugged into it.

○ You may want all lines to share the same phone number.
This is the best option, you don't want your users to have to
try several different phone numbers in order to connect.
Make sure that you talk to your phone service provider
(cable, Mercury, BT, etc) and find out if this is possible with
your phone, and how much it will cost.

Cables and connectors

This may sound like a silly sub-section, as it should be pretty
obvious. But I've included some other bits here also which
are of interest to BBS operators. As well as all the various
wires you will need to connect everything together, you
may also like to consider some mains power filtering and
protection. A computer is a fragile piece of machinery, and
is susceptible to spikes and surges on the mains electricity

supply. You can buy little surge and spike protectors which plug into an ordinary socket and offer some protection. Of course, these aren't going to save your BBS in event of a power-cut.

Power-cuts are nasty things. Not only do the lights go out, but so does the BBS. Murphy's law states that you won't be there to fix it all again when the power comes back on, as five minutes before the cut, you set off for two weeks holiday. Ensure your computer is configured to automatically reset and restart the BBS software when it is switched on. This will mean that at least your BBS should come "back on-line" if you're not there when the power returns.

Unfortunately, it has the potential to not be this straightforward. If the power cut occurred at a particularly bad time, when the hard drive was being written too, say, then things could be totally screwed up. If your budget permits, then it is worth having a look at UPSs.

A UPS is an "un-interruptible power supply". Basically, it is a huge battery in a box. When the power goes out, the battery cuts in and can give many hours of machine operating time depending on how much you spend. A £500 UPS should keep a BBS consisting of a PC and hard drive running for maybe 20 minutes.

Some UPSs have a special connector on the back which plugs into a computer and allows the computer to detect when a power cut has happened, and shut itself down accordingly. The catch with this great feature is that very little software, other than network servers, will take any

This is a diagram showing how everything fits together.

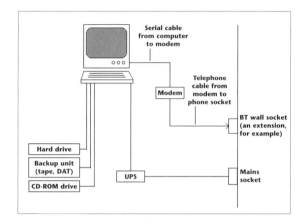

notice of this. 20 minutes is usually long enough to cover most power cuts.

If you are considering buying a UPS, then it is essential that you get further advice from a dealer. You will have to ensure that the one you buy is capable of supplying enough power to keep your setup going in event of power-loss, otherwise it will just shut itself down and be totally useless. Also, there are several kinds of UPSs, and different ones will suit different needs.

If you get power-cuts more than a few times a year, then a UPS moves out of the "luxury item" list and into the "I ought to have one of these, or I'll pay the price" list. Be warned!

Backup hardware

Computers don't always behave according to plan. Nor does the electricity supply, and power-cuts and spikes can wreak havoc with fragile electronic equipment. One way or another, sooner or later, something horrible will happen and your hard drive will be corrupted in some way. It could be because of the power supply, faulty software, or just a hard drive which has decided to pack in (they do, you know!). This can be a disaster, and I know of several BBSs which have had to close down for months, or even shut down completely, because all of their data was lost. The moral to this story, which most people ignore until they have their first hard disk crash, is to back up your data regularly.

The catch is, if you have 2Gb of data then you'll be needing a thousand floppy disks or so to back it all up. Of course, that is totally impractical. It would take days, and be tedious, expensive and has the potential to be unreliable – one disk could choose to go wrong, or you could lose one or two. The ideal solution is to buy a decent back-up system like a DAT tape drive. These are coming down in price, but a good one will still cost you near to a grand.

More often than not, you don't actually need to back up everything. Certain files, such as the files containing the usernames and passwords of all of your users, are more important than others, and should be backed up on a daily basis. A cheaper optical disk, storing about 128Mb on each disk, could be ideal for backing up chunks of data.

The software

You have two options, you can use someone else's BBS software or you can write your own. And the latter choice is much, much harder than you may think, even if you are a

competent programmer, so let's look at that option first as it is by far the most depressing.

Writing your own BBS software

I've tried this myself many times, and it is a project which I would not wish on anyone who didn't have a great deal of spare time. If you are thinking of this, then make a start now, and plan it in detail. Have a close look at chapter 2, and decide which services you wish to provide and try and figure out how you will provide them. If you are intending on supporting more than one user at once, your software will have to be able to do this.

You may think you can justify the development time by selling your software afterwards. It is unlikely you will make money out of this when it is finished for two reasons. The first is that it will never really be finished, and the second is that the market is crammed and yours will have to be exceptionally good to sell.

Normally, the only way you can realistically attempt this is if your BBS is going to provide a very specific closed service. In these cases, you may not be able to find software out there which will work for you, and you may not be faced with much choice. If you are going to go ahead with writing it yourself, keep these things in mind:

❍ Write it in a high level language you are familiar with, such as C or C++. Do NOT attempt to write it in assembly language, it will take years, and be hopeless overkill.

❍ Plan and document it in advance, and continue to document it as you are writing it.

○ Keep it as modular as possible to make future expansion and maintenance easier.

Using a currently available BBS package

Most privately operated BBSs provide the same kind of basic service. It is this which has provided the market for pre-written BBS software. The quality of this varies dramatically, and just because a package costs more does not necessarily mean that it will be best suited to your particular needs. Indeed, some of the best BBS packages are freeware or shareware, costing either nothing or very little to use. Before you choose it is worth looking at a number of options.

Using a pre-written BBS software package has a number of advantages. The first, and most obvious, is you don't have to write one yourself. In a lot of cases, they come with comprehensive setup and sysop control programs, making the process of running a BBS a whole lot easier.

Another potential advantage of using a pre-written BBS software package is that the interface which your callers will see is a standard one. (It might be said that this is a disadvantage, as all the BBSs using a particular piece of software will look the same. Chapter 5 talks about how to make your BBS unique.) Because of this standard interface, it is possible that an OLR can be used, which can cut down callers' phone costs considerably.

OLR stands for off-line reader. An off-line reader is a program which allows a user to read messages while not connected to the phone. The OLR will call a BBS, fetch any new messages, and then disconnect. The user then reads them at his/her leisure, perhaps leaving some new

messages or performing other actions. At a press of a button, the **OLR** will then call the **BBS** back, transfer any new messages and then disconnect. This can save a considerable amount of money, as callers are only on the phone for the minimum possible time. The **BBS** operator gains also; since users are not on the phone for very long, your system will be less clogged and easier to get through to.

As I have mentioned, the quality of BBS packages varies greatly, and that quality is not necessarily a function of price. To help you to find the right package for your BBS, here are some things you may wish to bear in mind when choosing. It is also worth checking out chapter 2, and making sure that the package you are considering allows you to either have, or add at a later date, the services you are thinking of providing to your users.

○ **Ease of setup.** Some shareware offerings in particular are a pain in the neck to set up. If you don't mind delving around altering numerous configuration files, then this may not be a problem. Most people, however, would rather select their modem from a list, press a few buttons, and get up and running for test purposes.

○ **Customisability.** If your BBS is going to look different from all the others, you are going to want to be able to customise it greatly. Almost all packages allow you to edit the menus, some allow you to design pretty menus yourself. Most allow you to add a dash of colour by using ANSI colour sequences, and provide a suitable page editor.

Lucy is an off-line reader for
Cix, on the Amiga.

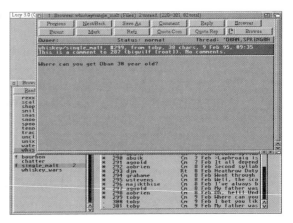

○ **Support for multiple lines.** Should your BBS become
popular, you'll possibly want to add more lines at a later
date. If this might be the case, ensure your BBS package
supports this. Also get an idea of how you may add this
support: If you're planning on simply adding a new card to
your computer giving you more serial ports, then your BBS
will need to be able to use them.

○ **Flexible maintenance programs.** BBS maintenance can
be very tedious. It involves many things, from checking new
files, tidying up messages, cleaning your hard drive of old
data, adding new users, sending messages and so on. Some
software makes this a more painful task than it need be.

○ **Network connections.** For connection to FidoNet, or the
Internet, you'll need support from the BBS software.

○ **Expandability.** If you are planning on adding games, or
other features to your BBS, you'll need some method of
doing this. Some BBS packages allow external programs to
be run, passing them a bit of basic information about the

current call (which serial port it's on, for example). These are often known as "doors" or "gates".

○ **Local log-ons.** You'll often want to log on to your own BBS and see exactly what the user would. This is important for testing, checking out new menus, and performing general BBS jobs.

○ **OLR support.** Some software provides OLR support (see above for more information on OLRs). If this is important to you, check the software allows it, and see what effect this may have on your ability to customise your BBS.

○ **Support.** Setting up a BBS can be a pain. If it all goes horribly wrong you may want somewhere to turn. If this is a concern for you, you may wish to consider buying a commercial package which entitles you to telephone support. A lot of the shareware packages provide limited support over Internet email, or Fidonet mail.

It is beyond the scope of this book to cover more than a handful of the available BBS software, but to give you some idea we'll briefly look at a couple of the options for the Amiga, PC and Macintosh:

Amiga BBS software

The Amiga has done very well for quality BBS software. This partly has something to do with the multi-tasking operating system, which is ideal for this sort of process. Most Amiga BBS software is capable of supporting many calls at once, most interface to Fidonet, and even allow Internet in some cases. (See chapters 2 and 4 for more information on

**DLG Professional, from a
sysop's point of view.**

```
Enter the letter of the menu entry to edit =) &

[ 1] Letter:  ..                    &
[ 2] Executable: (path/name)        doors:hackslash/Hack&Slash %Uname
[ 4] Description:                   Hack & Slash
[ 5] Type:                          Executable
[ 6] Help File:                     DOORS/&
[ 7] Lower level:                   1
[ 8] Upper level:                   255
[ 9] Hidden:                        NO
[10] Load type:                     OVERLAY
[11] Ask user if sure:              NO
[12] Pend messages:                 YES
[13] Cli mode:                      NO
[14] Pause on completion:           NO
[15] Log value:                     135
[16] Activity string:               Playing Hack & Slash
[17] Priority:                      DEFAULT
[18] Edit help file

Select =)
```

network connections.) The featured package is DLG
Professional, which is an excellent fully featured BBS
package. This is due for an overhaul now, and other
packages such as Excelsior are about to make a push into its
marketplace. It is also definitely worth checking out
XenoLink by Jonathan Forbes who can be contacted at:

1132 Bay Street

Suite 1101

Toronto, Ontario

M5S 2Z4 Canada

XenoLink 1.90 is a commercial product and costs $150,
with $15 P&P if ordered directly from the author. For more
information on Amiga BBS software, try calling around (see
chapter 7 for a few BBS names), consult the Usenet FAQ list
for BBSs (see the very end of this chapter), and if you have
Internet access, look at one of the AmiNet sites such as
ftp.luth.se in the pub/aminet/comm drawer. There is a sub-
drawer in here specifically for DLG, and the BBS drawer

contains more software to try as well as doors and
information.

DLG

Name:	DLG Professional
Cost:	Commercial Package. Costs about $160
Network access:	Fidonet and Internet
Contact:	Telepro Technology #20 – 1524 Rayner Avenue, Saskatoon, Saskatchewan, Canada S7N 1Y1
Demo BBS:	001 306 249 2352
Telephone (voice):	001 306 6653811
System requirements:	Any Amiga with at least Workbench and Kickstart 1.3. Works with minimal resource requirements.

DLG Professional is a very popular choice for Amiga sysops.
The current version, 1.0, is starting to show its age, and a
newer version has been expected for some time. Telepro say
that they are working on version 2.

It supports up to 65,000 users, and nearly 10,000 different
conference areas and file areas. It can support as many
nodes as there are serial ports. It can be heavily customised,
with all menus and text strings configurable by the sysop.

And **DLG** from a user's point of view. The excellent **Informatique BBS in Ireland** (see chapter 7 if you want to give it a call).

```
Now entering message area [1007]: Irish Amiga Echo

Total messages -> [200]
Msgs numbered -> [226 to 425]
New messages -> [199]

Area: [1007] [Irish Amiga Echo] [Message 226 of 425]

[Time Left: 115] Message Menu -> ?

CUGI Message Areas -- please leave some messages!
--------------------------------------------------------------
[RET] Show Next Ms  [E] Enter Msg      [A] Change Area   [N] Next Area
[B] Post Bulletin   [O] Edit Signature -[S] Change SIG   [P] Private Mail
[<] Reverse Read    [=] Cont Read      [I] Message Filter [J] Thread Toggle
[.] Header Scan     [T] Read Tagged    [U] List Readers  [^] To file area
[#] Reset Pointer   [&] TurboRead      [[] UnSubscribe   []] Subscribe
[W] QWK Bundler     [*] Scan Messages  [M] Main Menu     [H] Help
[?] Display Menu    [G] Goodbye
--------------------------------------------------------------

Area: [1007] [Irish Amiga Echo] [Message 226 of 425]

[Time Left: 115] Message Menu ->
                                   Z FC 8N1 38400  00:04:24 10:57 am
```

DLG supports Fidonet fully, and does not require any additional software in order to get connected. It comes with a front end mailer, TrapDoor (the most popular Amiga front end mailer). Internet support comes in the flavour of Usenet newsgroups only currently through the UUCP mechanism (Unix to Unix copy. UUCP is a method of getting Usenet mail and newsgroups, although these days most people get such information from a direct SLIP or PPP connection. See chapter 4 for more information on SLIP and PPP.)

Utilities are available to allow you to import Usenet messages from other databases, or provide further Internet connectivity, but this will require some work on the sysop's part. Most parts of the software are easily customisable, and you can even run external programs on messages before they are posted. (A possible one is automated filtering or conversion of messages, using, for example the excellent "jive" utility which converts English to jive.)

DLG comes with a nice manual in a ring binder, about 300 pages. The third party goodies brigade have came up with a great deal of doors, a mixture of shareware and freeware. These are available on DLG BBSs, or over the Internet.

PC BBS software

There are a multitude of BBS packages available for the PC, ranging from the free to the very expensive indeed. A great many commercial organisations use PCs running software such as Wildcat! for their support BBSs.

We are going to have a brief look at two of the most popular BBS packages for the PC, the aforementioned Wildcat! and RemoteAccess. Both are excellent, and it is recommended that you have a look at both before making any decisions, and speak to a few sysops who are using the software and see what they think. Also have a look around on the Internet, if you have access, or have a look at a bunch of other BBSs to see if there is any other software out there which may be of particular interest to you.

RemoteAccess

Name:	RemoteAccess
Cost:	Evaluation version available for free, as shareware. Registration costs £33.
	The shareware version only supports up to 2 nodes, but a commercial package is available which supports up to 250 nodes.

RemoteAccess
in action!

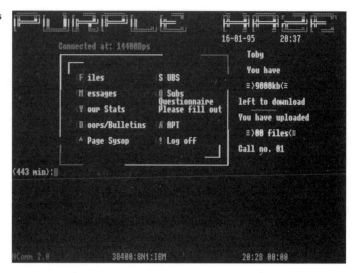

Network access: Fidonet and Internet

Contact: Registration/RA
FlightPath BBS
PO Box 268
Hounslow TW5 9PZ
Credit cards accepted (VISA and
ACCESS/Mastercard)

BBS: 0181 759 7775. **Fidonet:** 2:254/99

System requirements: IBM PC, MSDOS 3 and a FOSSIL
driver. FOSSIL drivers are packages
allowing communication between
communications software and a
Hayes compatible modem.

A relative latecomer in the PC BBS software field (1990), the popularity of RemoteAccess is growing rapidly. This is partially because of its cheapness, indeed, it costs nothing whatsoever to set up a BBS using RemoteAccess, and only £33 to register for the full version. The manual does say that you should register within three weeks having decided if it is the software for you, but at £33, even if it turns out not to be the software for you, it's hardly the greatest loss in the world! If you intend to run RemoteAccess from a commercial site (i.e. as a business's BBS) then you need to get the professional version.

A graphic user interface is available using the RIP (Remote Imaging Protocol) text based script language for users with terminals which support it. Everything is configurable, and made easy with flexible editors. (The language file editor makes it easy to add support for foreign languages, for example. I had the weird experience of viewing one RemoteAccess BBS in "jive". Sheit.)

I would definitely recommend having a close look at this software if you are planning on running a public access BBS.

Remote Access, setting it up to be used for the first time.

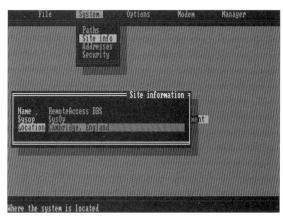

It is a bit of a pain to print out the manual, and it could certainly be better organised but the software itself is first class and a breeze to use. This is shown by the incredible variety of different types of BBSs which use RemoteAccess. There are a wide range of doors available, including a Tetris game which has to be seen to be believed (you can play against a user) and if you're a programmer it's easy to add your own doors to the system with the minimum of fuss.

Wildcat!

Name:	Wildcat! 4
Cost:	£116.33 for the single line version, including VAT.
	£217.38 for 10 line version, including VAT.
	(Both prices exclude delivery.)
Network access:	Fidonet, and some Internet with additional software.
Contact:	Mustang Software Inc. PO Box 2264 Bakersfield CA93303
BBS:	001 805 873 2400
UK support and sales:	Telesystems Ltd 3 Wycombe Rd Prestwood, Bucks, HP16 OND

The UK Wildcat!
support BBS in
action.

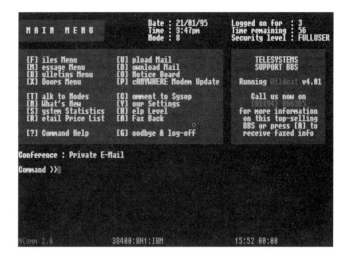

BBS: 01494 891903   **Tel**: 01494 866365

System requirements

Single line version: Pretty much any IBM PC with
640K of memory. About 15Mb of
hard drive space, a Hayes
compatible modem and MSDOS
3.3 or higher is required. I'd
personally recommend a 486 PC.

Multiline version: 386 processor, and 2Mb of RAM
for each dial-in line. Only 4 lines
per PC are possible.

Wildcat! claims to be the world's most popular BBS
software, so I guess it must be! It has been around for years
now, and a great deal of add on software, both free and
commercial, exists in the form of doors and utilities. It
supports multiple lines (so long as you buy a version for

more than a single line), Fidonet, and through an add-on package gives access to certain areas of the Internet. Wildcat! claims to be very secure against BBS misuse, which can be comforting. A graphic user interface is possible for access of the BBS by users using the standard RIP script language.

Wildcat! has powerful and flexible file management and conferencing, with up to 2 billion files in over 32,000 separate areas possible, and over 32,000 conferences. Mail can be linked with the Internet if the appropriate gateway package has also been obtained. The message system supports a full screen ANSI editor, and provides a built-in spell checker.

Sysop maintenance can be performed locally or remotely, and the sysop is able to log on to the bulletin board while callers are on-line. The system can be expanded by the sysop using a special development system which is available as an option from Mustang Software.

The documentation is excellent, a well put together 450 page bound manual explains all you need to know, including a good section on what it means to be a sysop.

Macintosh BBS software

The Macintosh is a strange one. The standard text only BBSs tended to be run from Amigas and PC's, but this hasn't stopped an excellent range of BBS packages appearing for it. The most common these days appear to be Telefinder and FirstClass. Both of these are expensive commercial products, and are designed to support point and click GUI's

for the users. The caller requires special software to take advantage of this, although in both cases, a text only standard interface can be used by callers without this software. We'll look at Telefinder in more detail, as that is the cheapest of the two and has great potential.

FirstClass was designed as a mail system, and is a collection of bolt together modules. It can be extremely expensive to set up a FirstClass BBS, prices of around a grand on software are figures you can expect to pay. Firstclass supports Fidonet, but it is complex to set up.

Telefinder

Name: Telefinder 3.2

Cost: £433.57 including VAT

Network access: Fidonet and Internet

Contact: AM Micro (UK Distributers)

Telephone (voice): 01392 426473

Telefinder from a sysop's point of view.

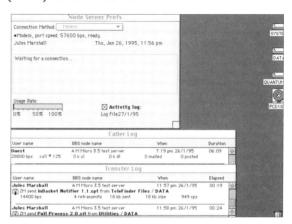

Telefinder from the users point of view, demonstrating the graphic user interface (GUI) as an alternative to straight text.

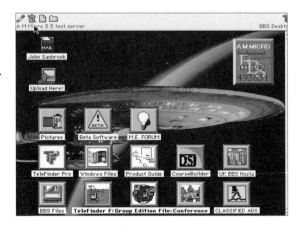

This is a bad time to write about Telefinder, because it is about to have a major upgrade. Version 3.5, which should be available by the time you read this, and contains significant enhancements (including the ability to connect direct to the Internet and accept calls via FTP!).

Telefinder supports Fidonet, but it is quite difficult to get set up. Macintosh BBSs don't appear to be so enthusiastic about Fidonet. Telefinder 3.2 (the current release) supports up to 32,000 users, and has no restrictions on conference and file counts. There is no limit to the number of nodes you can run from Telefinder 3.2, although the new update only allows you to run 2 nodes from the basic package, and you will have to buy additional nodes at a cost.

GUI client software (the replacement for a terminal, which the user uses to call your service) is available for the Macintosh and Windows, and users can also use a standard terminal to access your service in ANSI colour or standard text.

Further information

With hundreds of BBS packages available for MSDOS, Windows, OS/2, the Macintosh and the Amiga it would require another book twice this size to do justice to describing them all, and it would be out of date pretty soon after it was published. New packages appear all the time, and existing ones die, or get upgraded. If you are interested in getting more information on the software available, nothing can beat some of the documents and discussion groups on the Internet. If you have access to the Internet, particularly Usenet newsgroups, try subscribing to the following:

```
alt.bbs

alt.bbs.allsysop

comp.bbs.misc
```

A file of particular interest is the FAQ (Frequently Asked Questions) document for these groups. Weighing in at a hefty 360K, this lists details of most popular packages together with their specifications and contact details. You will find the FAQ interesting and informative.

Chapter 4
Networks

As mentioned in chapter 2, attaching to a large computer network is a good way of expanding your BBS without having to purchase much in the way of additional hardware (if anything) and providing your users with an improved, enlarged service. In this chapter we will look at the two major networks which are likely to interest BBS sysops in particular; the Internet, and Fidonet. We'll describe them both in more detail, and explain what you will need to do, and who you may wish to contact if you want to receive more information or connect up to them.

Fidonet

History and introduction

Fidonet was a clever plot hatched in 1984 by an American called Tom Jennings. He wanted to allow users of his BBS to be able to send messages to users of a friend's BBS. He wrote a program which would transfer messages sent to the other BBS late at night, when it was cheaper, and nobody was connected to his BBS. This expanded rapidly and by 1994, over 30,000 BBSs world wide were connected to Fidonet. At a regular pre-set time, they call other Fidonet sites (called nodes) and send data to other BBSs on Fidonet. In return, they receive more data back which may be for them, or need to be distributed further. This way, messages find their way to their destination by moving around from node to node. This can take a great deal of time, and messages are more prone to getting lost than they would be on the Internet.

Fidonet allows users to request files, as well as sending messages. This can make your phone bill grow, as your

.net Guide

Fidonet node will have to call others to move this information around.

Fidonet is very popular, and it is getting harder to find popular BBSs which are not Fidonet nodes. It gives users of your BBS access to a large amount of information that they would not otherwise see. This includes electronic mail, chatter on a lot of subjects (mostly computing related), and the ability to track down and receive files which you do not have.

Fidonet was created for BBSs, and it has evolved to meet the needs of BBS users and sysops. It is easy to see where the attraction lies, and it's a serious consideration if you are setting up a new BBS, particularly as almost all BBS software supports it. It costs nothing to become connected, and any other software required to make it all work is easy to come by, reliable, and is mostly shareware.

Addressing

A Fidonet address specifies each individual node on the network. If you wish to send mail to a user, or communicate with another node, you will need its address. They consist of four component parts, and work like postal addresses, each part helps to track down exactly which machine you wish to talk to. Here is an example Fidonet address:

```
1:234/567.8
```

It consists of four numbers. Left to right these are:

○ **Zone.** This is the first digit and normally refers to a continent. 1 means North America, 2 refers to Europe, 3 to the Pacific Rim (Australia, etc), 4 to South America, 5 to Africa and 6 to Asia.

○ **Region.** This helps to pinpoint where in the zone the destination BBS is. There are usually between 5 and 18 regions for each zone and a region spans a large geographical area. Regions are sub-divided into nets which are based on regional and technical considerations.

○ **Node.** This is the identifier for the actual Fidonet node number.

○ **Point.** Points are a further step down from nodes, and allow users of your BBS to effectively become part of Fidonet (see below).

When mailing someone on the Fidonet, you only need to know the final address. You do not have to be concerned with the route a message actually has to take in order to get there, the various nodes sort that out themselves from a node list. (This file is very large (over 1.5Mb) and contains the phone numbers and node information for each node on Fidonet. It is this information which allows crashmail to work, whereby you can cut out the middle men by calling the target machine directly.

How does it work?
Fidonet BBSs call each other in the early hours when phone call costs are cheap and a BBS is not normally busy. Packets of information are then moved around between machines on their journey to their final destination. Because this can involve a journey through many BBSs, information can often take days to arrive.

In order for all this to work, BBSs have to be able to support non-human callers, i.e. computers. This involves a piece of software which answers phones and decides whether the call is a human, or computer, and routes the call accordingly, called a "front end mailer". You'll often see this referred to as "trapdoor", or "frontdoor". (When logging on to many BBSs, you'll see the message 'Press ESC twice to enter the BBS'. You would then press escape twice and you're in. A computer caller would respond differently.) There are many such packages available, lots of the most commonly used ones are shareware and cost little to register. The front end mailer answers the call instead of your BBS package, and if it is a computer call then it will perform all the necessary data transfers.

As well as a front end mailer, you will also need a program which can then process any data received and feed that back into your BBS software. Such an application is called an "echomail processor". Such a program would have to be able to co-operate with your BBS, so check with BBS documentation to see what they recommend you use.

There are some other things worth mentioning about how Fidonet does its business. One of them is the ability to get things delivered quicker than normal by attempting to transfer directly with the destination machine. This type of transfer is called "crashmail". Most software supports this facility, but it can be expensive on phone calls as transfers may take place immediately and the call may be long distance. This kind of facility can be normally restricted to users of a certain security level.

The other interesting aspect is the issue of "points". A number of BBS users use their BBS solely for local access to

Fidonet, for electronic mail, file transfer and the Fidonet conferencing (echomail). By setting them up with a Fidonet point, they are able to use automated software to call your BBS, fetch any unread messages, and then disconnect. They can then read messages at their own leisure using an off-line reader and call you back later on to transfer any replies or new data. Allowing users to do this is entirely up to you, and they will need some special software (point software) in order to make use of the facility.

What if I am interested?

If you are interested in connecting to Fidonet, the first thing to check is that your BBS software supports it. It is unlikely that it will not. Also check what additional software you will require in order to make it work. Connection to Fidonet is free, and the best way to find out more information on obtaining a node listing is to contact your nearest Fidonet BBS sysop. See chapter 7 for some BBSs to call who are connected to Fidonet.

The Internet

History and introduction

The Internet was born in 1969 with the US military's ARPANET. It was created as a project to allow people working on different sites around the country to share relevant information easily. One of the other project goals was to get around the problem of conventional networks having a single central server. Should this get destroyed, then the whole network would fall over (in military terms this is a very serious consideration, communication in war time would be vital). ARPANET could survive any one of its

individual sites shutting down. It was designed to work in tatters (and some might say that the Internet, descended from ARPANET, does).

In December 1969 there were 4 machines on ARPANET. This grew rapidly, and the uses started to diversify, with users sending private email to each other, and swapping documents of interest (frowned on, but impractical to prevent due to the nature of the network). More networks throughout America began to connect to the ARPANET, with the National Science Foundation signing up in 1984. NASA, the department of health, the educational university networks and others were not far behind.

ARPANET officially shut down in 1989, having being split into two in the early 80s. The fledgling Internet's 30 thousand users at the time barely noticed, and growth continued exponentially into the 90s.

The Internet is also known as "the net", or the "information superhighway", the latter is not correct terminology, but the media love it. The information superhighway is not with us yet, but it certainly will be soon.

The Internet's greatest attraction is its size. At the last rough count 30 million people world-wide made use of the Internet on a daily basis, and it is currently growing at a rate of around 10% a month (pick up a calculator and work out the compound growth that will give for 1995 if you want a real shock).

Three million computers are all talking to each other 24 hours a day to move Internet information around. With this quantity of people, an incredibly diverse quantity of information has built up, and you can guarantee that no matter what you are interested in, the Internet is the place to find it.

The Internet's popularity has given rise to Internet mail becoming almost a standard now for international electronic mail. Commercial email services such as Cix, CompuServe, Delphi and many others have had to become connected to the Internet. A welcome side effect is that you can now send mail from any of these services to any of the others using this Internet gateway, and it is now possible to mail almost anyone who has any form of email service whatsoever using it. With this, and the array of information available, it is easy to see the attraction to BBS sysops.

The Internet has a nasty habit of becoming addictive to people, and as a side-effect quite expensive. The attraction is obvious, and you may want to seriously restrict the types of services you provide if the Internet is important to you.

Addressing

Each individual site on the Internet has a unique address which consists of four numbers, ranging from 0 to 255, separated with a single dot. These work in a similar way to postal addresses, and each number helps track down exactly where a given site is. The numeric form of addressing is particularly unfriendly, and addresses are normally referred to by a text alias. Lots of clever software (one piece of which is called a "domain name server", or DNS) sorts out the conversion of these text aliases to their numeric equivalents. Here is an example Internet address:

```
ben_n_angie@mum.co.uk
```

These addresses should be read from right to left to track down the actual location. After each stage, we will be a bit closer to our destination. The ".uk" bit indicates that this site is in the United Kingdom. This is often referred to as the top level domain country code. There are many others, such as ".ca" for Canada, and ".jp" for Japan for example. Sometimes this is not present, and in most cases this means that the site is in North America, but not always so.

The ".co" means that this site is a commercial organisation. In North America, this is usually seen as ".com" instead. There are others, such as ".edu" which means educational establishment, or ".gov" for government sites (NASA, for example, is a ".gov" site).

"Mum" is just an example standing in for the name of the commercial organiasation and "ben_n_angie" are the people I am trying to reach. The @ symbol simply means "at".

How does it work?

The Internet is made up of a number of computers which talk to each other using a protocol called TCP/IP. TCP/IP stands for "transmission control protocol/Internet protocol" and is the standard method for machines to exchange information on the Internet. The TCP bit of TCP/IP is responsible for converting information into special packets of data suitable for transmission. The IP part ensures that packets go to the right place. This could be a long way away, and packets may have to go through several machines before they reach their eventual destination.

There are two main ways of accessing the Internet, by direct TCP/IP connection, or by using a "shell account". A shell account is where you use a standard terminal program and modem to call your service provider, and then type in commands to access the Internet. This form of access can be hard to automate, which may be important to you if you want the whole thing to happen overnight for example.

A direct TCP/IP connection actually makes you part of the Internet while you are connected but does require more complex software. With this method, you run TCP/IP networking software on your own machine, and then route packets over a modem link using a protocol such as SLIP (serial link Internet protocol) or PPP (point to point protocol). SLIP and PPP convert TCP/IP packets to a form suitable to be sent over your modem, and at the other end they are converted back into TCP/IP packets.

Your service provider will usually provide you with software to do this, but you will have to check that it will all interface to your BBS software.

WARNING

The catch with the Internet is that it is a "live", or "on-line" service. In order to interact with facilities such as FTP and Telnet (see chapter 2) you have to be physically connected to your service provider. For your users to make use of this, you'll need two lines, and worst of all, you pay for the call to the service provider. The potential size of your telephone bill may give you kittens.

The easiest solution to this, which is adopted by most BBSs offering Internet support, is to restrict the services to those which can be conducted off-line such as Usenet newsgroups, and electronic mail. Your BBS simply calls the service provider late at night, and gets any new messages

and sends any which are waiting to be sent. This is all conducted automatically and can take as little as a few minutes depending on the amount of data which needs to be transferred. This method also cuts out the expensive need for a second line.

Internet features such as FTP obviously cannot be conducted in this manner, as they require interaction from the user. Be warned though, it is now possible to receive files via electronic mail. The user sends a specially formatted mail message to a certain Internet address. This is then decoded, and a requested file batched up, converted to ASCII data (usually UUENCODED) and sent back as email. As you can imagine, this could make for some seriously large email messages and you may wish to limit this kind of activity!

What if I am interested?

If you are interested, you'll need three things:

1. Software

2. A service provider

3. A BBS package which can support the Internet in some form, or allow access to other programs which can.

Most BBS software which supports the Internet does so in a limited way, usually offering just Internet mail and Usenet newsgroups (see chapter 2). Both of these Internet services do not require the BBS to be permanently connected to a service provider, and only require regular calls to move mail around and fetch new usenet messages and post any comments by your users. In order to actually do this you

#7 Setting up a BBS **.net**

will need a service provider. Before needlessly spending
money, check the documentation of your BBS package, or
ask a sysop who is already set up with the facility what he or
she needed to do. Most sysops I have come across are more
than happy to help with advice.

At your end you are going to need quite a complex
software setup, which is usually supplied by your service
provider for common machines, such as the PC, Macintosh
or Amiga.

UK service providers are springing up all over the place now.
Here are a couple and their contact addresses:

Demon Internet Ltd
42 Hendon Lane
London N3 1TT.

Telephone (voice):   0181 349 0063 (London)
or   0131 552 0344 (Scotland)

email: internet@demon.net

Demon Internet were the first company in the UK to
provide direct connection to the Internet to the general
public. Currently, they are also the largest with over 13,000
members. Connection is via SLIP or PPP and costs £10 +
VAT per month for access.

Future Connect
.net magazine
Beauford Court
30 Monmouth St.
Bath, BA1 2BW

Telephone (voice):   01225 442244

Future Connect is a relative newcomer. Registration to the service costs £50, and thereafter it costs £15 a month. The first year has to be paid in advance, which comes to £230 excluding VAT.

Chapter 5

Making your BBS unique

(or, how to make someone call your BBS)

With tens of thousands of BBSs available out there, one of the hardest parts of running one is actually getting anyone to call yours when there are so many others to choose from. In this section we'll take a look at some of the ways that you can make your BBS stand out from the others. There are no magic answers to making yourself popular though, it will involve a lot of work on your part in supporting it and keeping the pot boiling, so to speak.

If you are planning on running a private, closed BBS just for a few friends, then this section may not be too useful for you, but by far the majority of people setting up BBSs do so to get all sorts of people calling.

Creating your BBS can be the hardest part of the whole thing. It is relatively easy to get hold of the software and equipment that you need. Then you are faced with the awesome task of actually putting it all together; designing your conference and file areas for example. This tends to lead to sitting down in front of a computer thinking "um...okay, so what now?". The easy way out is to stick to defaults, and just get the service up and running. This is all well and good, but it hardly leads to a system which stands out from the others.

If you have decided to take the plunge, and set up and run your own BBS, then it is certainly worth the effort of sitting down with a bottle of wine (not obligatory), a pen and a lot of blank paper and doing some design work. It will save you a lot of grief in the long run, and you may be surprised what you come up with.

Why does anyone call a BBS anyway?

Good question. And there are many answers of course. Personally, I call BBSs when I need to get hold of some information or get questions answered. For that reason, there are only a few I call, which I know are the best ones to get what I want as quickly as possible. These days, as the Internet solves more of my problems I spend less time on BBSs, only calling those which are fun to be on, and which have the odd thing which is not on the Internet. It is also interesting to keep up with the BBS world and what is happening in it. This type of caller is very common, those who call, download a whole bunch of files, have a brief look around and then disconnect. They don't necessarily give very much back. (I'll give myself a slap later on for this outrageous behaviour.)

Other people call for different reasons. In some cases it is the social aspect, being involved in a group of like-thinking people and chatting about various subjects and swapping programs and data. BBSs can be an excellent way of distributing information. If you are a commercial organisation, or a computer user-group, then this can be a good way of getting newsletters and up-to-date items of interest directly to your target market.

For a lot of users, who do not use the Internet yet, BBSs can be the only way of keeping up with the latest gossip about what is happening in the computer world. Fidonet, for example, is very popular amongst Amiga users to discuss the fate of Commodore, and circulate the rumours and chatter. If your BBS carries these Fidonet discussions, then all of your users get access to them also.

Another bias towards the choice of which BBS to call is geographical location. For a lot of people who call BBSs, it is not financially possible to continually dial all around the country to get to services of interest, and most would much rather make a local call. One way of encouraging people to call your service rather than another, is to fill a gap in the market. Have a look at some of the BBSs in your area, and try and find out what other ones there are nearby. See what they don't cover, and that can be a useful lead as to where to start.

Advertising

Before we look at some ways of making your BBS unique to encourage callers to call back, there is one other issue that is certainly worth mentioning. Just setting up a BBS is not sufficient, of course, because if nobody knows about it, then you won't get any callers. One way to start is to advertise yourself on other BBSs (some sysops don't like this, so remember to ask first before advertising yourself on someone else's BBS). Another good way is to write in to computer magazines which do regular BBS and usergroup lists. It may be necessary to pay a small amount to leave such an advert, but it is a good way of banding your name and number around.

Once you have a caller, the trick is to make him or her call back, and preferably recommend you to a friend at the same time. (tel-a-friend, or word of mouth, is by far the best way of building and expanding your BBS).

A theme

Many bulletin boards have themes. A theme can be just about anything, there are bulletin boards out there which base themselves on all sorts of strange subjects, from Elvis to the Hitchhikers Guide to the Galaxy. You don't have to go this far, but it's certainly worth the effort of developing a character for your BBS. You can do this in the presentation, see below for more on that.

Name your BBS something interesting. "ZBBS-Cambridge" is hardly an interesting name, so come up with something which sums up your BBS as best as it can in a few words. If you were thinking of starting a BBS which themed on pinball tables, then you might call it "extra ball" or something like that. There is little doubt what the BBS is about, and you could draw some neat ANSI graphics of pinball tables and the such.

To take this theme of pinball a bit further, and to demonstrate how you can construct a BBS around it, you may for example have the following discussion groups (conferences):

○ `computer_pinball` For discussion of computer pinball games, such as Pinball Fantasies. The file area for this may contain demo versions of these products, and some cheats and hint files.

○ `old_tables` Chatter about how it used to be, with the rotary score counters, and all that other hideous stuff which most people were glad to see the back of! (In my opinion, of course!)

○ `modern_tables` Chat about modern tables. File area may contain GIF pictures of table playfields, with files showing what everything does. Files with cheats and hints for these tables may also be here.

○ `latest_and_greatest` All things new and wonderful. People can talk about the newest ones available and argue about how good they are.

○ `williams_v_de` Arguments about who is best, Williams tables, Data East tables and Bally. (Williams of course.) Files could include which tables are made by which manufacturer.

○ `tables_for_sale` Pinball table sales. You can buy real second hand pinball tables for a few hundred pounds. Many companies exist to sell them to individuals. This area would be for price lists and tables available. Users could sell their tables here too. File list may include currently available tables from certain companies.

○ `pinball_lounge` The lounge area. That nice quiet area full of people drinking and talking about pinball when they should be out enjoying a social life. I ought to take more notice of this myself of course!

It is easy to see that with such a theme, in a few hours, you can sit down and design the structure of your BBS and guarantee that it is going to be different from everyone else's BBS. You could then use your theme when designing your menus. If you are drawing in ANSI, or making use of a GUI method of accessing BBSs (such as those offered by RemoteAccess on the PC, and Telefinder on the Mac, see

towards the end of chapter 3) you can then come up with some cool stuff.

Theming your BBS is not compulsory, and indeed not necessary. Many BBSs do very well out of the fact that they are extremely well presented and have an enthusiastic sysop. (See presentation below).

Covering a unique subject better than everyone else

If your bulletin board is especially for users of Amigas then you can try to make your BBS particularly useful for Amiga owners, by providing up to date news and information, or a good range of files. This can also relate to theming as we discussed above, although they are not necessarily connected. You could have a BBS which concentrated on the Amiga specifically, but was laid out and presented to look like something out of "Aliens". With our pinball idea above, though, the two are very closely linked. The theme is also our main subject matter, and will dictate how the whole service appears to the user.

It is worth noting that creating a BBS which covers a subject matter in the computing field, and making it stand out, can be very hard for two reasons. The first is that there are bound to be other BBSs out there covering the same thing, and who have been doing it a lot longer that you. The second is the amount of work required by yourself to ensure that you do have the latest information.

Having a chat with one of the poor sysops who was conned into answering questions for me.

If your BBS focuses on PC shareware, for example, you have to get a whole lot of the latest shareware to start with, and then ensure that it is updated regularly – as you cannot rely on people to keep uploading stuff, especially at the beginning. People call BBSs for a number of reasons, and if yours is a computer related service then they are probably going to call to get hold of software. If you have none at the outset, then they are unlikely to call back.

Good presentation and an enthusiastic sysop

The most important ingredient you can add to your BBS is enthusiasm and patience. As I said earlier, think of it as a plant, look after it well, and you'll eventually see the results of your work, but it is not instantaneous. Don't expect 1,000 callers in your first week, for example, unless you're very lucky indeed!

A particularly pretty **ANSI**
main menu for the **Sound**
and **Vision** BBS. If you want
to call it up, look in chapter
7 for the number.

A lot of a user's impression of your service will be down to
the way in which it is presented. It is astonishing what you
can do with a little imagination and ANSI graphics.

I have been amazed at the quality of some of the menus I
came across during the research of this book, ranging from
the beautiful to the extremely odd indeed. Since the menus
are in general the way in which users will communicate
with your BBS, it makes good sense to spend quality time
designing and laying them out.

The degree to which this is customisable will depend greatly
on the BBS software which you are using. Some have
limited options when it comes to menu design and this
tends to lead to a lot of BBSs which look pretty much the
same. At the same time as making things pretty, ensure that
you don't lose contact with the real world. Your BBS should
be as easy to use and navigate around as possible.

There are a number of smaller things which you can do to
make your BBS more attractive to callers. One is foreign
language support. RemoteAccess BBS software for the PC

Sheit man. Jive. Quite
definitely my favourite
custom option on a BBS.

```
a short questionaire. Upon completion you will have 40 minutes online as well
as a download ratio of 150 K per day. This may not seem alot, but there are
certain files which are FREE. The idea is to give you an idea of what is
available on Airtel so that you consider Subscribing.

The Subscription idea is not to make me a rich man, but to help me break even
on the costs of running Airtel. After all £15.00 per annum equates to less than

Why not have a £80.00 [Once Only payment] LIFE MEMBERSHIP subscription
which is great value for money. [UNLIMITED TIME/DOWNLOADS]

Enjoy the system, if you have any comments, please don't hesistate to contact
me by leaving a message.

Adrian Pop  (Sysop)

Would ya' likes ANSI colour and graphicsY [Y/n]? Ya

Do ya' wants t' use de damn ANSI full-screen edito'Y [Y/o]? Ya

Would ya' likes AVATAR codes t' be sentN [y/N]? Na

Use de damn full screen message viewa'Y [Y/o]? Ya

How many lines duz yo' display gots (10-66, 24 recommended):24

Would ya' likes t' pause afta' each screen pageY [Y/n]?
[Com 2.0                    Adrian Pop                    21:31 00:01
```

allows all of its prompts and messages (700 of them) to be
customised into different languages, and callers then get to
pick the one of their choice. This may sound silly,
particularly as you are probably not expecting a flurry of
calls from Sweden, but it can be used to add a bit of
personality to your BBS.

One such BBS I called gave me the option of viewing menus
in jive instead of English. I can't remember laughing so
much for a long time! There is a potentially serious side to
this also. You can have several versions of the English
language stuff, one containing brief terse messages for
more advanced users, and one containing more detailed
verbose ones for beginners.

MAKE A
NOTE!

**There is nothing more irritating to a BBS caller than a
sysop who is obviously not interested in helping users
out, and joining in with the service. If you don't think
you'll have the time to offer a great deal of support, then
try and think how you can get help.**

A lot of sysops alleviate this problem with the help of one or more co-sysops, who are there to help operate the service, register users, and keep everything up to date, neat and tidy. You may wish to rope a friend or two into helping you. A little enthusiasm can go a long way, particularly when it comes to welcoming new users to your service and getting to know them. One BBS I know of, for example, refuses to register new users and allow them access until the sysop has phoned the user and had a chat first. This leads to a friendly atmosphere, as the sysop sort of knows everyone, and the users in particular know the sysop.

Lots of lines

I've mentioned it last, because it is the one you'll almost certainly implement last. If your BBS becomes popular, then it can become frustrating for users to connect because your phone line is always engaged. Frustrated users who have difficulties getting through regularly may not call again. The way around this (other than permanent direct connection to the Internet which, as we've already discussed, is very expensive) is to have more than one phone line, preferably sharing the same telephone number so users don't have to try several lines to find the one which is available.

WARNING
Most BBS software supports more than one line these days, but with some commercial packages you will have to pay additional money for a licence to do this. Also be warned that some BBS software also needs more than one computer once you go over a certain number of lines, and requires some serious memory resources to achieve this.

Chapter 6
Legal issues

If you're a regular watcher of Roger Cook on the TV, you may remember the episode about child pornography on BBSs. Some unsuspecting sysop had his door broken down in the early hours and all his equipment stolen. He was in a great deal of trouble indeed, and still attempted to claim he knew nothing about the data in question.

In this section we'll have a look at three of the main legal issues, illegal software distribution (software piracy), illegal data (pornography, some drug and terrorism issues), and the Data Protection Act and see what they could mean to you.

WARNING

Since this is one of the sections I suspect most readers will turn to quite quickly for various reasons, it is definitely the place to briefly preach to you and also mention computer security briefly. Using your BBS for illegal purposes is likely to get you placed up a certain creek without a paddle, life raft, and with your canoe on fire. The fraud squad, computer crime squad and pornography squad are getting a lot better at tracking down offenders, and if you are caught, you may never see your BBS hardware again. And worse still, you are likely to get a criminal record which will be with you for the rest of your life. Which is another reason why this section is so important. If you are aware of the law, and where you stand, then there is less chance of you getting into a pickle.

Security

Hackers are familiar to us all. We've all seen "Wargames" (and if you haven't, go out and hire it, it shows its age but gives an insight into how hard people can try to break into a computer system) where a high school kid hacks into a communication service and has a crack at destroying the world (unintentionally of course!). It is still an issue. There are people out there who will try very hard indeed to break into BBSs and attempt to cause damage, and you should be aware of this issue. Encourage your users to use sensible passwords to avoid their accounts being misused, and make sure you check that your BBS software provides the security you need.

The legal stuff

Illegal software distribution

You are all aware of software piracy. This involves the distribution and use of commercial software without permission from the authors. Most people, sadly, are guilty of this at some point in their lives, but with BBSs and other forms of electronic communications it comes into a whole new world, literally. Software can be pirated in a far off country, and the results distributed world-wide in a matter of hours. This is, of course, illegal and there are bodies in this country responsible for tracking down and prosecuting offenders.

Software piracy is illegal. You could be detained at Her Majesty's Pleasure for up to 2 years, and/or receive a nasty fine. As I mention below in the section on illegal data, you can do your best to claim ignorance to any illegal stuff on your BBS, but it is going to be very difficult to convince a court of law that you were unaware of it being there.

Illegal data

The term 'illegal data' covers the electronic distribution of anything which is illegal, which does include software piracy, but I've separated the two, software piracy is dealt with above. For our purposes, we are going to talk about illegal data in the form of material which is classed as illegal for various reasons, excluding software piracy. This does include, however, a great deal of pornography, information on drugs, some documents which discuss terrorism issues (how to make a bomb, for example) and some other data also.

Certain data, particularly a lot of pornographic material is illegal in this country. This is covered by certain legal documents which are cheap and easy to obtain. It is certainly worth obtaining these and having a good read if you are planning on allowing any form of "adult" data on your BBS.

○ **Obscene Publications Act 1959** This costs £1.50. The penalties for criminal behaviour covered by this act can be up to 3 years in prison, and/or a hefty fine.

○ **Protection of Children Act 1978** This costs 25p. Breaking parts of this can give the same sorts of penalties as for the Obscene Publications Act.

○ **Section 160 of the Criminal Justice Act 1988** The entire document costs £11.80. This section covers the possession of indecent photographs of minors.

○ **Criminal Justice and Public Order Act 1994** The document costs £18.00. This has only recently become law, and clarifies points of law in the Obscene Publications Act with regards to computer images.

These documents are available from HMSO (Her Majesty's Stationary Office). HMSO accept credit card orders, or will invoice for payment. They accept VISA, ACCESS or American Express. VAT is not payable on any of the documents, and delivery is about 7 days. To order any of these documents (or the Data Protection Act 1984 which is also available) you can phone **0171 873 9090**

If you wish to make general enquiries about documents, you can phone **0171 873 0011**

The Data Protection Act

The Data Protection Act 1984 was created for your benefit. It is there to prevent companies moving your personal information about without your permission, or you knowing about it. It can also cover BBSs, which is why you should be aware of it. For legal reasons you may find yourself needing to store real names and full addresses of your users. Depending on what purpose your BBS performs, or what you intend doing with that data, you may be required to register with the Data Protection Act Registrar.

The Data Protection Act is a complex beast. If you wish to get hold of the entire text, you can obtain it from HMSO. (See above for the contact number for them.) It is complex in that there are certain exclusions which mean that you may not have to pay any money. Briefly, if you are intending on sharing the names and addresses you store with other people, or your BBS has *any* commercial activities on it whatsoever, the chances are that you will have to register, and pay. If your BBS is entirely recreational, and your users give direct permission for you to store the data, then you may not have to pay any money at all. The best advice is to phone the enquiry line, they are extremely helpful.

Some guidance for BBS operators is currently being prepared. This should be available by the time you read this. If you wish to get more information, or wish to find out how the Act affects you, you can either write or phone.

Enquiries Line   **01625 535777**

ODPR, Wycliffe House, Water Lane, Wilmslow, FK9 5AF.

Registering costs £75 for 3 years. This is regardless of the number of purposes you are planning on using any stored data for.

Remember the Data Protection Act is for your personal, and your users' protection. It means that you are able to control who gives your name and address away, and people holding names and addresses are forced to disclose exactly what they are going to do with them. If you are not sure how it may affect you, phone the enquiry line and ask.

Chapter 7

Some bulletin boards to try

Welcome to the end of the book. If you've got here then you're either at the beginning, wanting to try out a few BBSs, or at the end checking out this footnote. In both cases you will have realised that there is more to setting up a BBS than simply getting some software and hardware together, plugging into a phone line and starting straight away.

Running a BBS causes your wallet to become emptier, it also requires time and enthusiasm in order to succeed. You may also realise that this book doesn't cover the whole issue in total detail. That would have been impossible, as new BBS software appears all the time, and things can change so much.

Hopefully we will have been able to give you a fair idea of what is involved, give you some leads and the basic information you need to get started, as well as covering the all important legal issues in the previous section.

Remember that for any BBS which is open to the public, you are there to provide a service to your users. If they do not feel that you are doing that, they simply won't call back again. Treat your users with respect, co-operate with them, and be prepared to be flexible to meet their needs.

All that remains is for me to say good luck, and have fun! If you get your BBS up and running as a result of buying this book, drop me a line, and I'll give it a call. My Internet email address is:

```
toby@cix.compulink.co.uk
```

A few **BBS**s to check out

To get you started, here are a handful of BBSs that you may like to try out. You'll find that on a lot of BBSs, an alternative list of numbers that you may wish to try is given when you disconnect, which can provide further leads.

Empyrion
Amiga and PC. Based on PC software.

Number: **01792 580781**

Sysop   David Westron

An excellent BBS, with wide network support including Internet newsgroups and email. The sysop is very helpful and the BBS is well put together and managed.

Informatique
Amiga based using DLG Professional.

Number   **00 353 1 872 1232** (Ireland)

Sysop   Eddy Carroll

A well run and well put together BBS using DLG Professional on the Amiga. Informatique is the longest running Irish Amiga BBS. The sysop is the famed and helpful Eddy Carroll, who wrote the essential SnoopDOS tool.

Airtel
PC based using RemoteAccess

Number   **01342 717800**

Sysop   Adrian Pop

A good example of a well set up RemoteAccess BBS. This
one is pilot orientated and carries a lot of CAA and other
pilot materials (including the relevant Fidonet groups). This
BBS is the one which amused me with Jive as a language
option. Other mysterious language options include Star Trek
speak, would you believe it! Worth a call as an example of a
RemoteAccess BBS and to see how BBSs can cover specialist
subjects well (see chapter 5).

Amiga Junction 9
Amiga based using DLG Pro

Number   **01372 271000**

Sysop   Stephen Anderson

Popular Amiga BBS with Internet mail and usenet news
access available to users as well as the normal collection of
Fidonet goodies. Amiga Junction 9 has more than one line

Amiga Junction 9 welcomes me back for another visit.

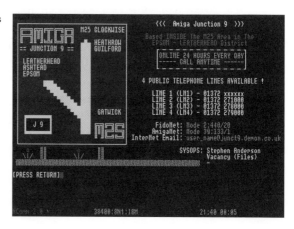

Getting the option to download the client software to use the **GUI** (graphic user interface) rather than the (rather difficult to use) Telefinder **ANSI** and **ASCII** menus.

```
Please type "MMM" to log on...

TeleFinder
MM

Welcome to Mac Jungle BBS Line 1!
It's now 9:54:42 pm, on 29/1/95.

(L) Logon to the BBS.
(R) Register as a new user.
(D) Download TeleFinder/User for Macintosh.
(W) Download TF/User for Windows.
(G) Goodbye (Disconnect).

[WELCOME] ? )
NComm 2.0           38400:8N1:IBM              21:49 00:05
```

including private lines for BBS members. An impressive collection of files and goodies for the Amiga user.

Mac Jungle

Mac based, using Telefinder

Number	**01235 520507**
Sysop	Jules Marshall

Good place to check out a Telefinder BBS, and download the special GUI client software for Windows or the Macintosh to see what a difference that can make.

Primal Disorder

PC based using RemoteAccess

Number	**01628 74179**
Sysop	Tim Mole

The sound half of Sound
and Vision. Obviously.

The source of heaps of pretty ANSI graphics and menus.
The sysop says that he formed the BBS because he was
bored, and there were no other decent BBSs in the area.
He's not done badly!

Sound and Vision
PC based using RemoteAccess

Number   **01932 252323**

Sysop   Rob Barth

Not surprisingly, biased towards sound and vision! Yet
another excellent RemoteAccess BBS, this one is a
commercial venture where you are asked to donate towards
an already massive hardware setup. It has thousands of
members, and massive storage capacity on both hard disk
and CD-ROM. Internet mail and Usenet news are
supported.

.net Guide

Chapter 8

Reference

Smiley Dictionary

It can be very difficult to express emotional content within a plain text message, and very easy to interpret a message the wrong way. A system of "smileys" (or emote-icons for any of our American friends reading this) has been developed and is now in widespread use. A smiley is a small face made of standard characters, (turn the page sideways if you still don't 'see' them), and can help convey feelings ranging from sad to mad to glad. There are also now smileys to cover much more than just these standard emotions, and as you can see from this dictionary they are not all to be taken too seriously.

Smiley	Meaning
:-||	Angry
(:-)	Bald
:-)	Basic happy
:-(	Basic sad
B-)	Batman
:-)>	Bearded
%+(	Beaten up
?-)	Black eye
:-)X	Bow tie
R-)	Broken glasses
:^)	Broken nose
|:-)	Bushy eyebrows
)	Cheshire cat
<|-)	Chinese
3:-)	Cow
:-t	Cross
X-)	Cross-eyed
:'-(	Crying

i-)	Detective (private eye)
:-e	Disappointed
:-)′	Drooling
{:V	Duck
<:-)	Dumb question
5:-)	Elvis
>:-)	Evil grin
:‴-(	Floods of tears
:-!	Foot in mouth
/:-)	French
8)	Frog
::-)	Glasses wearer (1)
8-)	Glasses wearer (2)
8:)	Gorilla
:-′)	Has a cold (1)
:*)	Has a cold (2)
:-|	Hmmmph!
:-C	Jaw hits floor
.-)	Keeping an eye out
:-#	Kiss (1)
:-*	Kiss (2)
:-X	Kiss (3)
:+)	Large nose
:-D	Laughing out loud
:-}	Leering
(-:	Left-handed
:-9	Licking lips
:-}	Lipstick wearer
:- |	Monkey
:-{	Moustache (1)
:-#)	Moustache (2)
(-)	Needs haircut
:^)	Nose out-of-joint
:8)	Pig

:-?	Pipe smoker
=:-)	Punk
:-"	Pursed lips
|-]	Robocop
O:-)	Saint
:-@	Screaming
:-O	Shocked
:-V	Shouting
|-)	Sleeping
:-i	Smoker (1)
:-Q	Smoker (2)
:-j	Smoker smiling
:-6	Sour taste in mouth
:-v	Speaking
:-w	Speaks with forked tongue
*-)	Stoned
:-T	Tight-lipped
:-p	Tongue-in-cheek
:-&	Tongue-tied
:-/	Undecided
:-[	Vampire (1)
:-|<	Vampire (2)
:-<	Vampire (3)
:-)=	Vampire (4)
:-))	Very happy
:-((	Very sad
:-c	Very unhappy
C|:-)	Wearing bowler hat
d:-)	Wearing cap
[:-)	Wearing headphones
:-(#)	Wears teeth braces
;-)	Winking
:-7	Wry smile
|-O	Yawning

Acronym Dictionary

Because time equals money, and never more so than in the world of on-line communications, people have devised ways of saving typing time by reducing common phrases into acronyms. These are known as TLAs, or Three Letter Acronyms, although many are not truly acronyms at all and very few actually have three letters. Oh well, such is life. There is a whole lorry-load of these TLAs around, and I dare say that I have missed some. But I hope that this dictionary will cover the ones that are in most common usage and it should go a long way to help you make sense of some seemingly senseless terms.

Acronym	Meaning
AFAICT	As Far As I Can Tell
AFAIK	As Far As I Know
AFK	Away From Keyboard
AIUI	As I Understand It
B4	Before
BAK	Back At Keyboard
BBL	Be Back Later
BCNU	Be seeing you
BRB	Be Right Back
BSF	But Seriously Folks
BST	But Seriously Though
BTDT	Been There Done That
BTSOOM	Beats The Shit Out Of Me
BTW	By The Way
BWQ	Buzz Word Quotient
CLM	Career Limiting Move
CUL	See you later
DWIM	Do What I Mean

DWISNWID	Do What I Say Not What I Do
DYJHIW	Don't You Just Hate It When...
ESAD	Eat Shit And Die
ETLA	Extended Three Letter Acronym
EOF	End Of File
F2F	Face to Face
FAQ	Frequently Asked Question
FFS	For Fucks Sake
FOAD	Fuck Off And Die
FOAF	Friend Of A Friend
FOC	Free Of Charge
FUBAR	Fucked Up Beyond All Recognition
FWIW	For What It's Worth
FYA	For Your Amusement
FYE	For Your Entertainment
FYI	For Your Information
<G>	Grin
GA	Go Ahead
GAL	Get A Life
GIGO	Garbage In Garbage Out
GR&D	Grinning Running & Ducking
HHOJ	Ha Ha, Only Joking
HHOS	Ha Ha, Only Serious
IAE	In Any Event
IANAL	I Am Not A Lawyer
IBN	I'm Buck Naked
IIRC	If I Recall Correctly
IMBO	In My Bloody Opinion
IME	In My Experience
IMHO	In My Humble Opinion
IMNSHO	In My Not So Humble Opinion
IMO	In My Opinion
IOW	In Other Words
IRL	In Real Life

ISTM	It Seems To Me
ISTR	I Seem To Recall
ITRO	In The Region Of
ITRW	In The Real World
IWBNI	It Would Be Nice If
IYSWIM	If You See What I Mean
JAM	Just A Minute
KISS	Keep It Simple, Stupid
L8R	Later
LOL	Laughs Out Loud
MFTL	My Favourite Toy Language
MORF	Male Or Female?
MOTAS	Member Of The Appropriate Sex
MOTOS	Member Of The Opposite Sex
MOTSS	Member Of The Same Sex
MUD	Multi User Dungeon
MUG	Multi User Game
NALOPKT	Not A Lot Of People Know That
NFWM	No Fucking Way Man!
NIFOC	Nude In Front Of Computer
NRN	No Reply Necessary
OAO	Over And Out
OBTW	Oh, By The Way
OEM	Original Equipment Manufacturer
OIC	Oh, I See
OMG	Oh My God
OTOH	On The Other Hand
OTT	Over The Top
PD	Public Domain
PITA	Pain In The Arse
POD	Piece Of Data
RFD	Request For Discussion
ROFL	Rolls On Floor Laughing
RSN	Real Soon Now

RTFAQ	Read The FAQ
RTFM	Read The Fucking Manual
RUOK	Are you OK
SITD	Still In The Dark
SMOP	Small Matter Of Programming
SNAFU	Situation Normal, All Fucked Up
SNR	Signal to Noise Ratio
SO	Significant Other
SOL	Shit Outta Luck
STFU	Shut The Fuck Up
TANSTAAFL	There Ain't No Such Thing As A Free Lunch
TCB	Trouble Came Back
TDM	Too Damn Many
TIA	Thanks In Advance
TIC	Tongue In Cheek
TLA	Three Letter Acronym
TNX	Thanks
TPTB	The Powers That Be
TTFN	Ta Ta For Now
TTYL	Talk To You Later
TVM	Thanks Very Much
UBD	User Brain Damage
VC	Virtual Community
VR	Virtual Reality
WIBNI	Would It Be Nice If
WRT	With Regard To
WTF	What The Fuck
WTH	What The Hell
WYSIWYG	What You See Is What You Get
YABA	Yet Another Bloody Acronym
YHBM	You Have Bin Mail
YHM	You Have Mail

Jargon busting

One of the things that I have always found most annoying when reading books on any specialist subject is that the author oftens assumes a degree of technical knowledge, with regard to jargon, on the part of the reader. I don't assume, nor would I expect, that the readers of this book will be aware of every term used in this book. Therefore I have compiled what I hope you will agree is a very handy and comprehensive glossary of Internet and Comms terminology. If I have done my job properly, and there is a first time for everything folks, then you should be able to locate any word that you are unsure of here and find its meaning.

Glossary

ACK	An acknowledgement number carried in the TCP header that tells a TCP sender the sequence number of the byte which the TCP receiver expects next.
Address	Either the address of a user of a system, as in an email address (required so the message sent can be directed to a particular person) or the address of a site on the Internet.
AFS	A set of protocols, similar to NFS, that allow for the use of files on another network machine as if they were on your local machine.

Analogue Loopback   A modem self test which tests the
                             modem's originate or answer
                             frequency.

Analogue Signals   Continuous but varying
                             waveforms, an example being the
                             voice tones transmitted over a
                             telephone line.

ANSI   American National Standards
                             Institute, responsible for
                             approving standards in many
                             areas.

Anonymous FTP   Anonymous FTP allows a user to
                             retrieve files from another site on
                             the Internet without having to
                             establish a userid and password
                             on the system.

Application   A piece of software that performs
                             a useful function.

Arc   To create a compressed archive of
                             a file, or group of files, using the
                             PKARC compression program.
                             Now very dated, but many arc'ed
                             files are still to be found on the
                             Internet.

Archie   A system for finding publicly
                             available files for FTP over the
                             Internet.

Archive	A file, or group of files, that have been compressed to form one smaller file. Depending on the program used to compress the archive, it will bear one of many file extensions, including .lha .zip .arc .zoo .tar
ARPA	Advanced Research Projects Agency, part of the United States Department of Defence.
ARPAnet	The experimental network upon which the Internet was based.
ARQ	Automatic Repeat Request. An error control protocol used by Miracom modems.
ASCII	American Standard Code for Information Interchange. A code supported by just about every computer manufacturer to represent letters, numbers, and special characters.
Asynchronous	A form of data transmission which allows information to be sent at irregular intervals.
Bandwidth	The difference in Hertz between the highest and lowest frequencies of a transmission channel. Usually

used to describe the amount of
traffic through a particular
newsgroup or conference.

Bang Path   An old UUCP email address
                         system.

Barf   A failure to work!

Baseband   A digital signalling technique used
                         in Ethernet local area networks.

Baud   Unit of measurement denoting the
                         number of transitions in modem
                         signals per second. Each transition
                         may carry more than one bit of
                         information.

BBS   Bulletin Board System.

Bigot   A common character type found
                         in Cyberspace.

Bit   A unit of measurement that
                         represents one character of data.
                         A bit is the smallest unit of storage
                         in a computer.

BITNET   An IBM based academic computer
                         network. BITNET is an acronym for
                         "Because It's Time, NETwork"

Bits Per Second   The speed at which bits are
                         transmitted.

Blinking	Using an Off Line Reader to access an online system.
Block	Data consisting of a fixed number of characters or records, moved as a single unit during transmission.
Bogus	Non functional, or not nice.
Bounce	When email is returned due to a failure to deliver.
Bridge	A device that connects two or more physical networks and forwards packets between them.
Broadband	A transmission method often used to send different kinds of signal at the same time, like voice and data for example.
Buffer	A memory area used as a temporary storage device for data during input/output operations.
Byte	A group of binary digits that are stored and operated upon as a unit.
Cable	A bunch of insulated wires with end connectors, an example being a serial cable.

Carrier
A signal of continuous frequency capable of being modulated with another information carrying signal.

CCITT
International Consultative Committee for Telegraphy and Telephony. An organisation that produces international technical standards for data communications. Has recently been replaced by the ITU-T.

Cello
A World Wide Web graphical browser program for Windows users.

Character
A binary representation of a letter, number or symbol.

CIM
The CompuServe Information Manager is the officially supported off line reader and system navigator for CompuServe.

CI$
See also "CIS". The dollar sign replaces the "S" in this slang version, due to the cost of using the service.

CIS
CompuServe, the American online information service.

Cix	Compulink Information eXchange. The largest conferencing system in the UK.
CIX	The Commercial Internet Exchange, an agreement amongst Internet Service Providers regarding the commercial use of the Internet. Not to be confused with the Compulink Information eXchange although it quite often is as they share the same acronym.
Cixen	People who use the Compulink Information eXchange.
Client	An application that extracts information from a server on your behalf.
CommUnity	The Computer Communicators' Association, set up to protect and further computer communications in the UK. Similar in aims to the EFF, but with a UK perspective.
COM	A code in MS-DOS that refers to a serial port.
Compress	A UNIX archiving program that "compresses" the size of a file.

Conference	A message area, or forum, on a conferencing system like CIX. Each conference covers a defined subject matter, and is further subdivided into topics of more specific subject matter. For example, there may be a Sooty conference which has topics of Sooty, Sweep, and Sue.
Connect Time	The length of time you spend on-line to the Internet.
Cookie	A random quote, generated by software. Found on many online systems.
CoSy	CoSy is the operating system that online services like CIX and BIX are based upon. It is a shortening of the words "Conferencing System".
CPS	Characters Per Second. A measurement of data output speed.
Crash	A sudden and total system failure.
CRC	Cyclic Redundancy Checking. A type of error detection.
CREN	The Corporation for Research and Educational Networking, which

was formed by a merger of
BITNET and CSNET.

Cross post   To post the same message to
more than one conference,
message area, newsgroup.

CTS   Clear To Send, an RS-232C signal
that basically means that
everything is OK for transmission
of data.

Cyberpunk   A person who "lives" in the future
culture of Cyberspace, Virtual
Reality etc. As epitomised by the
works of Bruce Sterling.

Cyberspace   A term coined by William Gibson
in his novel "Neuromancer" used
to describe the collective "World"
of networked computers. Now
commonly used to refer to the
world that exists within computer
networks, accessed by comms
technology. My favourite
definition is simply "the electric
domain".

Daemon   A program which sits on a system
waiting to automatically perform a
specific function. Daemon is an
acronym for "Disk and Execution
MONitor".

#7 Setting up a BBS .net

DARPA	The Defence Advanced Research Projects Agency, responsible for the development of ARPANET which was the basis of what was to develop into the Internet.
DASD	Direct Access Storage Device.
Data Compression	The compression of information to decrease transferred file size. MNP5 and V.42bis are the best known types.
Datagram	The primary unit of information transferred over the Internet using the Internet Protocol.
DCE	Data Communications Equipment.
Decryption	Decoding encrypted data to its original form.
Dial-Up	To connect to another computer by calling it over the telephone network.
DIP Switch	Dual Interface Poll switch which enables the user to set various parameters of a circuit board (commonly found on modems and printers).
DNS	Domain Name System is a database system for translating

	computer domain names into numeric Internet addresses.
Domain	Part of the naming hierarchy of the Internet.
Domain Name Server	Domain Name Servers enable domain names to be resolved into numerical IP addresses.
Down	Not working, as in "the BBS is down".
Download	The transfer of a file from another, remote, computer to your computer.
DTE	Data Terminal Equipment.
DTR	Data Terminal Ready, an RS-232C signal that is part of the handshake in a data transmission interface.
Duplex	A communications channel capable of carrying a signal in both directions.
EARN	European Academic Research Network.
EFF	Electronic Frontier Foundation, an American organisation that addresses the social and legal

issues arising from the increased use of computer communications.

EMACS   One of the most common editors found on online systems.

Email   Electronic Mail. A method of sending messages via computer instead of the usual land based postal system. One of the most popular and important uses of computer communications.

Emote Icons   See "Smiley".

Encryption   A method of coding data to prevent unathorised access, most commonly used on the Internet to protect Email from prying eyes.

Equalisation   A compensation circuit built into some modems to offset distortion caused by the telephone channel.

Error Control   A variety of different techniques which check the reliability of characters or blocks of data.

Ethernet   A type of high speed local area network.

EUNet   European UNIX Network.

FAQ	A Frequently Asked Question. You will find FAQ files all over the Internet, in Usenet Newsgroups, mailing lists, at FTP, Gopher, and WWW sites. You'll even find an FAQ section in this book!
File Server	A computer that stores files on the Internet, making them available for access by Internet tools.
Finger	A program that displays the user, or users, on a remote system.
Firewall	A firewall is a security device to help protect a private network from Internet crackers and hackers. It is a machine with two network interfaces that is configured to restrict what protocols can be used across the boundaries and to decide what internal IP addresses can be seen to the external Internet.
Flame	An abusive or personal attack against the poster of a message. A flame is the online equivalent of losing your rag or thumping your teapot.
Flow Control	A technique to compensate for the differences in the flow of data input and output from a modem.

Fortune Cookie   See "Cookie".

Forum   A message area on CompuServe or
                          Delphi, equivalent to an echo on
                          Fidonet, a newsgroup on USENET,
                          or a conference on CIX.

Fragmentation   The process by which an IP
                          datagram is broken into smaller
                          pieces, so as to meet the
                          requirements of a specific
                          physical network.

Frame   A block of data with header and
                          trailer information attached.

FreeNet   A popular method of providing
                          "free" access to the Internet from
                          the United States. Probably the
                          most famous being the Cleveland
                          FreeNet, which was also the first.

FTP   The File Transfer Protocol that
                          defines how files are transferred
                          over the Internet.

Full Duplex   Flow of information in both
                          directions at the same time.

Gateway   A computer system to transfer data
                          between otherwise incompatible
                          networks.

Gibson, William	Author of "Neuromancer". Responsible for coining the term "Cyberspace".
Gopher	A menu based system for exploring the Internet.
Hacker	Someone who enjoys exploring computer systems, often applied to people who undertake such explorations illegally.
Half Duplex	Flow of information in both directions, but one way at a time.
Handshaking	An exchange of signals allowing communication between two devices, designed to start or keep the two in synchronisation.
Hayes	A modem manufacturer responsible for the first direct connection modems, and whose command set has become the industry standard.
Header	Part of a packet which precedes the actual data and contains source, destination, and error checking information.
Host	A computer that allows users to communicate with other computers on a network.

#7 Setting up a BBS **.net**
the internet magazine

Hostname	The name given to a host computer.
HST	High Speed Technology. A proprietary signalling scheme used as part of the trademark for Miracom HST modems.
HTML	HyperText Mark-up Language, the language used to write a World Wide Web document.
HTTP	HyperText Transfer Protocol, used extensively by World Wide Web. Another of the many Internet protocols.
Hub	A device connected to many other devices.
Hz	Hertz. A measurement of frequency, each unit being one cycle per second.
IAB	The Internet Architecture Board, the "head honchos" if you like, who make decisions about Internet standards.
ICMP	Internet Control Message Protocol is the group of messages exchanged by IP modules in order to report errors.

Internet	Worldwide network of computer networks, connected using the IP protocol.
Internet Society	An organisation that exists to support the Internet, and also the governing body of the Internet Architecture Board.
IP	Internet Protocol on which the Internet is based.
IRC	Internet Relay Chat allows many users to chat in real time across the Internet.
ISDN	Integrated Services Digital Network combines voice and digital network services in one medium.
ISN	Initial Sequence Number is the first sequence number used on a TCP connection.
ITU-T	International Telecommunications UnionTelecommunications. The Telecommunications standards making organisation, which replaces the CCITT.
JANET	The Joint Academic NETwork of educational establishments in the UK.

JUNET	Japanese UNIX Network.
KA9Q	An implementation of TCP/IP for amateur packet radio systems.
Kermit	A file transfer protocol named after Kermit the Frog!
Kernel	The system commands containing level of an operating system or network system.
Kill File	A file which filters out any messages posted by those people named in it. If someone is in your kill file, you never see any messages from them again, hence you have effectively killed them. Seen in great numbers on USENET but also implemented in a growing number of Off Line Readers for various online systems.
Kit	Computer equipment.
Knowbot	The Knowbot Information Service is another method of trying to find where someone dwells within the Internet.
LAN	Local Area Network. A data network that serves a small area only.

Leased Line	A permanent connection between two sites, which requires no voltage on the line and no dialling.
LED	Light Emitting Diode. A device that emits light when electrical voltage is applied to it. Used on modem front panels as status indicators.
Line Noise	Disruption of computer communications caused by interference on the telephone line.
Lion Nose	See "line noise",
LISTSERV	An automated mailing list distribution system.
Local Echo	All transmitted data is sent to the screen of the sending computer.
Log	A record of file operations. In comms use, the storing to disk or file of an on-line session.
Login	The process of identifying yourself on an online system. Generally a two stage process involving the input of your username followed by your password.

Login Name	The "username" or name of your account used for identification purposes.
Lurker	Someone who reads but doesn't post in newsgroups, conferences, or message areas. A sort of online voyeur.
Macro	A macro instruction is a string or instruction replaced by a shorter string or instruction. In use this means you can execute a long sequence by typing just a short one.
Mail Gateway	A machine that transfers mail between two or more email systems.
Mailing List	A discussion group whose messages are distributed by email.
MHS	Message Handling System.
MILNET	The US MILitary NETwork.
MIME	Mulitpurpose Internet Mail Extensions, a method of linking binary code into email.
MNP	Microcom Network Protocol is a common modem error correction system.

Mode	A specific condition or state under which a device may operate.
Modem	MOdulator/DEModulator. A device to convert binary information into an analogue signal that can be transmitted over normal voice carrying telephone lines, and convert that signal back into computer readable data at the other end.
Moderator	The person who runs, or moderates, a conference or message area.
Mosaic	Probably the most commonly used World Wide Web graphical browser. Has been developed for many platforms, including Windows, Amiga, X-Windows, and Macintosh.
MTU	Maximum Transmission Unit is the largest unit of data that can be sent on a given system.
MUD	Multi User Dungeon, an online role playing adventure game.
MUG	Multi User Game, any online game where there are two or more players at the same time.

Net

Generally used as another name for the Internet, although sometimes people refer to both USENET and Cyberspace in general as "The Net".

Netfind

A service that helps find email addresses for people on the Internet.

Net God

Someone who has achieved a "Godlike" status on the Net, either through the development of part of the Net or tools used in it, or because of their presence on the Net.

Net Police

A derogatory term applied to those people who feel it is their duty to tell others how they should behave in Cyberspace.

Net Surfer

Someone who "surfs" the Internet, wandering around looking for interesting places to visit, interesting files to grab, and interesting people to talk to.

Netiquette

The supposed etiquette of the online community, examples being avoiding overuse of quoting, avoiding cross posting, and so on.

Network	A group of computers that can communicate with each other.
Newbie	Someone who is a newcomer to a USENET group, often used as a term of ridicule or abuse.
Newsgroup	A message area, defined by subject matter, which forms part of USENET.
NFS	The Network File System. This allows use of files on remote network machines as if they were on your local machine.
NIC	Network Information Centre.
Node	A computer attached to a network.
NRAM	Non-volatile memory used by such devices as modems to store a user definable configuration which is read and acted upon at power up.
NSFNET	The National Science Foundation Network is one of the networks that makes up the Internet.
Null Modem	A cable used to directly connect two computers by their serial

	ports in which the transmitting and receiving pins are swapped.
Numeric Database	A database containing, specifically and unsurprisingly, numbers.
Offline	Not connected to an online system.
Off Line Reader	See "OLR".
OLR	Off Line Reader. A program that enables you to connect to an online system, download all your messages and email, read and reply to the offline and then send back your replies. An OLR can save you lots of money in telephone bills and online service charges, as well as provide in some cases a better user interface to the online system.
On-line	Refers to when two computers are connected by means of modems. For example, a Bulletin Board System is also an Online System.
Originate Mode	When the modem transmits in frequencies which are the reverse of the modem being called which is in answer mode.
Packet	A bundle of data.

Parity Bit	A check bit added to a unit of data for error checking purposes.
Password	A security string that is required to be input before access to a system, or part of a system, may be granted.
Phreaking	Making phone calls whilst bypassing the charging system. Phone phreaking was the forerunner to hacking as we understand it today.
PING	Packet Internet Groper is a program used to test destinations on the Internet to see if they exist, are operating, etc.
Plonk	The sound a newbie makes as he plummets to the bottom of a killfile list in a USENET group.
Pointer	A file marker so that an online system can remember what messages you have read when you disconnect, so you don't have to read them all again next time.
Polling	Connecting to another system to check for email and messages etc,
Port Number	Computers which run the TCP/IP protocols can use different ports

to run different services. Each of these ports is allocated a specific number. Local services tend to be assigned on higher port numbers.

Post

To send a message, either by email or to a conference, message area, or newsgroup.

Postmaster

The person responsible for taking care of mail across the Internet.

PPP

Point to Point Protocol. This allows a computer to use TCP/IP with a standard telephone line.

Profile

A control file for a program. Most commonly used to set up a user's individual preferences when logging onto an online service.

Protocol

Standards governing the transfer of information between computers. Developed to improve the reliability and speed of data transfer.

Public Domain

Software which is available to anyone without the requirement to pay for it.

Remote Echo

Everything the remote computer transmits is duplicated on your computer's screen.

REN	Ring Equivalent Number refers to a total figure which must not be surpassed by equipment connected to a single telephone socket.
REN and STIMPY	Happy Happy, Joy Joy.
Resume	A text file containing personal information about a user of an online system, usually written by the user themselves.
RFC	Request For Comments are sets of papers used for discussion on Internet standards.
ROT-13	A simple form of encryption, commonly applied to some USENET messages, which rotates the alphabet 13 places forwards or backwards.
Router	A system that transfers information between two networks using the same protocols.
Scratchpad	A temporary file used to hold messages whilst awaiting transfer or editing. Used on some online systems such as CIX.
Serial Cable	The cable used to connect devices through a computer's serial port.

Serial Port	The port that transmits and receives asynchronous data. Peripheral devices such as modems, printers, and mice can all use the serial port.
Server	A computer, or the software on that computer, that allows other computers to use it by means of client software.
Service Provider	Any organisation offering connections to the Internet, or part of it.
Shareware	Software which is generally available as "try before you buy" with the available version needing to be registered before its full power can be unleashed.
SIG	Special Interest Group, a forum or collection of forums on a particular subject. Found on on-line systems such as Delphi and CompuServe.
Signal to noise ratio	Used to describe the amount of on-topic postings as compared to the amount of wibble within a message area or conference.
Signature	A personal tag line used on the end of messages posted to online

services. These can vary from a couple of words to many lines in length. Also known commonly as "sigs".

Site   Any of the individual networks that, as a whole, comprise the Internet.

SLIP   Serial Line IP is a protocol that allows a computer to use the Internet protocols using a standard telephone line.

Smiley   A smiling face character made by joining ASCII characters together. Used to express emotions etc. See the "Smiley Dictionary" in this book for more details.

SMTP   Simple Mail Transfer Protocol is used to transfer email between computers, as part of the TCP/IP protocol family.

Snail Mail   The sending of mail using the traditional land based postal system as opposed to email. So called because of its slowness compared to electronic mail.

Start/Stop Bits   Bits attached to a character before transmission during an asynchronous transfer.

Sterling, Bruce	Author mainly responsible for the coining of the term "Cyberpunk".
SysOp	SYStem OPerator, the person who runs a Bulletin Board System.
TCP	Transmission Control Protocol. One of the protocols upon which the Internet is based.
Teapot	One of my favourite words.
Teledildonics	The sexual act performed with the aid of Virtual Reality, computers, telecommunications and a couple of very sad and lonely people indeed.
Telnet	An Internet protocol that allows you to log in to other computer systems on the Net.
Thread	A series of postings to a message area or conference that are linked together. A thread consists of an initial posting followed by all the comments to it, and forms an online conversation or debate.
Throughput	The amount of data transmitted per second without the overhead of protocol information.

TLA	A Three Letter Acronym, although these are often found to contain more than three letters. Used to minimise typing and speed up communications. See the "TLA Dictionary" in this book for more details.
Topic	A subdivision of a conference, where the subject matter has been more distinctly defined. See entry for "Conference" for more details.
UDP	User Datagram Protocol, another of the protocols upon which the Internet is based.
UNIX	An operating system commonly used across the Internet.
Upload	The sending of a file from your computer to another, remote, computer.
URL	Uniform Resource Locator, an attempt to standardise the location or address details of Internet resources. Most commonly used, at the moment, in connection with the World Wide Web.

USENET	A group of systems that exchange debate, chat, etc in the form of newsgroups across the Internet.
UUCP	Unix to Unix copy is used for copying files between Unix systems.
UUencode	A method of encoding binary data so that it can be sent as an ASCII file across networks by Email. A decoder is required to convert the file back into an executable binary file again.
V.21	An ITU-T standard, a modem speed of 300bps.
V.22	An ITU-T standard, a modem speed of 1200bps.
V.22bis	An ITU-T standard, a modem speed of 2400bps.
V.23	An ITU-T standard, sending data at 75bps and receiving data at 1200bps.
V.32	An ITU-T standard, a modem speed of 9600bps.
V.32bis	An ITU-T standard, a modem speed of 14400bps.

V.34	An ITU-T standard a modem speed of 28800bps.
V.42	An ITU-T error correction standard.
V.42bis	An ITU-T error correction standard with data compression.
Veronica	An Internet tool that provides a Gopher menu that matched your keyword Gopher search.
Video Display	A monitor to those not talking techno-babbleTerminal.
Virtual Circuit	A logical transmission path.
Virtual Communities	A term that describes the communities that are very real, but exist only in computer networks. Another name for Cyberspace.
Virtual Reality	A computer technology that creates a very real illusion of being in an artificial world. Virtual Reality has already found its way into many real-life applications, from chemistry to architecture to games.
Virus	A program designed to infect and sometimes destroy other programs and computer equipment. Virus

programmers are known, politely, as SMEEEEEEEEEEEEEEGHEADS.

WAIS   Wide Area Information Servers are used for searching databases across the Internet.

WAN   A Wide Area Network as opposed to a Local Area Network.

White Pages   A list of Internet users, accessible through the Internet itself.

Whois   An Internet program to find out the Email address etc of someone from a given name.

Wibble   Nonsense posted to a message area, conference, or newsgroup. Made into an art form by the likes of talk.bizarre on USENET and the norman conference on CIX.

World Wide Web   A hypertext based information and resource system for the Internet.

WWW   See "World Wide Web".

X.25   A packet switched data network, which is usually half-duplex.

X.29   The command set used to
                             configure and establish X.25
                             connections.

X.400   An ITU-T standard for Email
                             formats.

Zip   To archive a file or group of files
                             using the PKZip archiver.

Index

.net Guide

Other Internet books
from Future Publishing

This books forms part of a series of 12 Internet guides published by Future Publishing. Each guide is targeted at a specific type of Internet user, and explains everything you need to know about using the Internet for your own specific purposes.

We also publish an umbrella Internet title called 'All you need to know about the Internet', which costs £14.95 and comes with a free disk containing Chameleon Sampler, a demo suite of Internet software for PC owners. 'All you need to know about the Internet' is the perfect reference guide for newcomers to the Internet. It introduces all the activities you can engage in on the Net, including email, newsgroups, mailing lists, file transfer and much, much more.

All of these books are published in conjunction with Future Publishing's brand new UK-based .net magazine, which contains features for both experienced net users and newcomers. It features very high production and editorial quality, and is an essential source of information for those discovering the Internet's amazing potential. Retailing for £2.95, it's available at all good newsagents.

Future Publishing is committed to providing the best possible coverage of the Internet, which we believe is the computing revolution of the decade. Part of this coverage is this series of .net Guides, each targeted at specific Net users and needs. Each .net Guide consists of between 150-200 pages, is sized at 220mm (H) x 150mm (W) and retails at £7.95. Here is a list of all 12 titles:

 .net Guide

.net Guide #1
All you need to know about Getting On-Line
by Toby Simpson
How to get on the Net quickly, easily and cheaply. No
nonsense, no jargon, no hassle.
ISBN 1-898275-31-9
Publication Date December 1994

.net Guide #2
All you need to know about Communicating On-Line
by Davey Winder
Do you know 3 million people? You do now. Find out how
to talk to people all over the world.
ISBN 1-898275-32-7
Publication Date November 1994

.net Guide #3
All you need to know about Using the Net
by Davey Winder
The Net software is your gateway to a world of information.
Find out how to really use it.
ISBN 1-898275-33-5
Publication Date November 1994

.net Guide #4
All you need to know about Teleworking
Simon Cooke
No commuting, no rush-hour… no boss? Find out how to
work from home via the Net.
ISBN 1-898275-34-3
Publication Date March 1995

.net Guide #5

All you need to know about On-Line Information

by Eddy Robinson

Forget your local library. The Net is the biggest source of information the world has ever seen. Find out how to get it.

ISBN 1-898275-35-1

Publication Date March 1995

.net Guide #6

All you need to know about Mailing Lists

by Davey Winder

Don't go searching for information – make it come to you. Keep up to date on anything from poodles to particle accelerators.

ISBN 1-898275-36-X

Publication Date February 1995

.net Guide #7

All you need to know about Setting up a BBS

by Toby Simpson

Find out how to run your own on-line service. What it costs, what to avoid – and how to make it a success.

ISBN 1-898275-37-8

Publication Date March 1995

net Guide #8

All you need to know about On-Line Gaming

by Davey Winder

Games consoles are history. Discover real gaming with real people in real situations. On-line gaming is the future.

ISBN 1-898275-38-6

Publication Date February 1995

.net Guide #9
All you need to know about UK Internet Service Providers
by Davey Winder
You need a Service Provider. Find out who offers what and for how much.
ISBN 1-898275-39-4
Publication Date February 1995

.net Guide #10
All you need to know about The World Wide Web
by Davey Winder
Compare colour TV with long-wave radio. That's the World Wide Web compared to the standard Net interface. Believe it.
ISBN 1-898275-40-8
Publication Date December 1994

.net Guide #11
All you need to know about Business On-Line
by Davey Winder
Good business is all about communication, expertise and commercial awareness. Find out how the Net will give you the edge.
ISBN 1-898275-42-4
Publication Date February 1995

.net Guide #12
All you need to know about Internet Jargon
by Davey Winder
Baffled by jargon? Hacked off with technical terms? Every Internet buzz-word is explained right here. In plain English.
ISBN 1-898275-43-2
Publication Date February 1995

#7 Setting up a BBS **.net**

To find out the latest on availability and prices, call our order hotline

☎ **01225 822511**

 .net Guide